A NEW DICTIONARY
FOR EPISCOPALIANS

A NEW DICTIONARY
FOR EPISCOPALIANS

John N. Wall, Jr.

Illustrations by
Philippa J. Goodwin

Harper & Row, Publishers, San Francisco
Cambridge, Hagerstown, New York, Philadelphia
London, Mexico City, São Paulo, Singapore, Sydney

Cover design: Art Direction Inc.

Library of Congress Catalog Card Number: 85-51010

ISBN: 0-86683-787-6

Printed in the United States of America

5   4   3

Foreword

Who better than George Herbert to remind us that in the ordinary is to be found the extra-ordinary? Herbert wrote of the Holy Scripture that "when it condescends to the naming of a plough, a hatchet, a bushell, leaven, boyes, piping and dancing," it shows that "things of ordinary use are not only to serve in the way of drudgery, but to be washed, and cleansed, and (to) serve for lights even of Heavenly Truths."

John Wall's *New Dictionary for Episcopalians* is a handy, impeccably researched guide that illuminates ordinary things (and some not ordinary at all) and lets us see them in the context of the heavenly truths they serve.

Many other books have been written commenting on words, symbols, and signs. Dr. Wall defines them from A to Z—or, in biblical parlance, from Alpha to Omega. While most of the listings are not essential, they are important as the outward and visible portions of our experience in church and in our spiritual study.

I am grateful to Dr. Wall for having defined and explained the *vestments* I wear each Sunday and the *crosier* I carry. With the help of his *New Dictionary for Episcopalians*, when you enter your church's *narthex* and walk down the *nave* to take your seat in a *pew*, you will, in a very real sense, know more precisely and fully where you are. It is enriching to know, as you look up from opening prayer, that you are seeing priests wearing *albs*, or perhaps a bishop in *rochet* and *chimere*, as they go to the *altar* and open the *missal*.

The author addresses the book both to Episcopalians and to those who are outside the Episcopal Church but who wish to learn the terminology of its liturgy, architecture, clothing, and organizational structure. The work certainly fills a need for the Episcopal Church, about sixty percent of whose members have come to our faith from other denominations.

As with all dictionaries, some of the content will be more pertinent than others. For example, you may never have seen an *abbot* or a *verger* (I do hope you will see many *altars* and *pews*), but Dr. Wall's alphabet will prepare you for the experience, should it arise. My hope is that at least some of the words that Dr. Wall has washed and cleansed will "serve for lights even of Heavenly Truths."

Robert Whitridge Estill
Bishop of North Carolina

INTRODUCTION

This book is intended to be a way of learning about the Episcopal Church. In writing it I have, of course, had newcomers in mind. I was once a newcomer to the Episcopal Church—a number of years ago. It seemed that everyone else knew when to stand, when to kneel, and when to sit. The people I met were very friendly, but they talked so easily about chalices and crucifers. They knew the difference, apparently, between cassocks and chasubles, while I was lost amidst lots and lots of new words I did not recognize.

Later I found out what all those words mean, and, as one who makes his living dealing with words, I also learned that the special words the Episcopal Church uses come from its rich and ancient heritage. But the rich heritage of language and the many diverse places it comes from also make it difficult for someone new to the church to know what is going on and being talked about. The Prayer Book has many English words in it, and lots of them are unfamiliar. It also has Latin words and Greek words and Hebrew words. The buildings the church builds, the services of worship it conducts, and the clothes people wear to conduct them also have names unfamiliar to people who did not grow up as Episcopalians.

For a long time I was bothered by the barrier between oldtimers and newcomers that all these special words create. Later I realized that knowing those words helps us identify our heritage as Episcopalians. Finally I decided that when people share a life together, they will inevitably come to have a language in common. That shared experience and language attract new members.

At the same time, however, the church must not be a secret society. We can use and enjoy the language that reveals our community life, but we must explain it to others so that they can enter into that life with as much ease and sense of belonging as possible.

That, really, is what this book is all about. In it I have tried to bring together all the words for the services of the church, its vestments, its buildings, and its organization that might interest, puzzle, or confuse the newcomer. I envision this book being used as a resource, over and over again, as new words are encountered. I do not imagine anyone reading it through from beginning to end. In fact, to do that would give the reader an odd perspective on the church.

I do want to make four things clear about the content of this book:

1. The Episcopal Church is heir to many diverse traditions, some ancient and some more recent, which shape what it does and how it does things. I have tried to incorporate as much as possible from many traditions, always in the knowledge that no parish community reflects every tradition, or even the same parts of every tradition. I hope that people encountering the Episcopal Church in different parishes will find here what they need to understand what is going on; they can simply ignore what they don't need to know now, secure in the knowledge that if they move to another parish they may find they need all those other words. However, parish practices aren't always easily defined. There is a parish in my city which conducts worship very simply, but it has a tabernacle on the altar, a feature associated usually with parishes with a rich and colorful liturgical life.

2. The Episcopal Church in the Book of Common Prayer and its companion volume, the Book of Occasional Services, offers opportunities for expressing liturgically moments of significance in peoples' lives which may go unobserved. I have tried to point out some of these services. A House Blessing according to the rite set forth in

the Book of Occasional Services can be a splendid way to get one's neighborhood, parish community, and other friends together. The Prayer Book's section of Prayers and Thanksgivings gives prayers for almost every occasion and situation. The Blessings over Food at Easter in the Book of Occasional Services can enrich family prayer life. The list could go on and on. Get a Prayer Book and look through it. Ask the rector to lend you a copy of the Book of Occasional Services. Then you will be prepared in advance when the occasion arises.

3. For the most part, I have stayed away from theological matters. But I have expressed a theology: that the Episcopal Church is a pragmatic church in which the life we live together, enabled by the Book of Common Prayer, is more important to us than doctrinal agreement or similar personal experience. To that end, I have defined those practical things that enable an institution to function. These include the governing structure of a parish, of a diocese, of a province, and of the national church and the Anglican communion. I have discussed words employed when a parish chooses a new rector and when it makes decisions. So, ask your rector about the doctrine of the Trinity; look here for a list of Episcopal seminaries or diocesan committees.

4. I have not spent much time in trying to say *why* we do certain things. Obviously, there are strong and powerful reasons for doing the basic things we do. We celebrate the Eucharist because Jesus told us to and because over the course of two thousand years that has proven to be essential to knowing what it means to be a follower of Christ. For other things like why we have vestries and both suffragan and coadjutor bishops, the reasons involve long stories of development and the perception of needs and solutions that are too long to recount here. For other things like why clergy wear ropes around their middles with albs, the reasons are long lost in customs of dress and fashion and the profound conservatism of the church

as an institution which preserves something important
about itself by keeping things like that going over two
thousand years. Most of the "reasons" one runs into for
things like that are apologetic and involve forced symbolism which no intelligent adult should be forced to endure.
In any case, I intend to help people identify and have
words for what they are curious about so that they can
ask about it if they want to. The point of all this is to help
you find what enriches your experience of the basic
things, not to load you down with explanations that may
not be very helpful.

After I started work on this book, I found, also, that lots
of people who are longtime Episcopalians don't know what
all the terms are for people, organizations, and things. So I
expect that this book will be of interest to many who are not
newcomers, or who are newcomers to only some aspects of
the life of the Episcopal Church. All are welcome to use it
as they will. I have given page numbers in the Prayer Book
(BCP) and the Book of Occasional Services (BOS) to help
the reader locate the things defined in this book. I have also
considered the possible frustrations of using a dictionary,
and tried to avoid making the reader jump around all over
the place. But the need to be economical with space means
that not every strange word is defined every time it is used.
So, if a word in a definition is itself unfamiliar, look for it in
its own alphabetical location.

For further reading, I recommend what have been con-
stant companions for me in doing this book. The most helpful has been *The Oxford Dictionary of the Christian
Church* in both its full and concise versions. Marion Hatch-
ett's *Commentary on the American Prayer Book* (Seabury,
1980) is a veritable treasure house of information about the
background and development of Christian worship, especially in regard to the Prayer Book. Dennis Michno's *A
Manual for Acolytes* (Morehouse-Barlow, 1981) and *A
Priest's Handbook: The Ceremonies of the Church* (Morehouse-Barlow, 1983) present in clear detail one style of

ceremonial in keeping with the Prayer Book. His work will clarify and improve use of the Prayer Book, regardless of whether or not one wishes to follow that style in every detail.

Basic texts everyone ought to know about, besides the Book of Common Prayer, include several books published by the Church Hymnal Corporation: *The Hymnal,* The Book of Occasional Services, *The Daily Office Book, Lesser Feasts and Fasts,* and the *Episcopal Clergy Directory.* Also basic is the *Episcopal Church Annual* (Morehouse-Barlow). There are almost too many Episcopal publications to mention any. I will probably hear from someone whose favorite is left out, but certainly everyone ought to know about *The Episcopalian* and *The Living Church,* two publications for general readers which have lots of news and reviews. Many of the seminaries have more scholarly journals, and there are also publications by most of the religious orders. For a full list, see the *Episcopal Church Annual* section on church periodicals.

I must here give special thanks to a number of people who have had much to do with my getting this book done. Harvey Guthrie, Lloyd Patterson, and John Booty taught me at the Episcopal Theological School (now the Episcopal Divinity School) that getting to the basic purpose of something in the life of the church was to go a long way toward understanding it. Keith Reeve, the rector, and all the parishioners at St. Mark's Church, Raleigh, have taught me what a Christian community can be. My bishop, Robert Estill, has helped me understand the full meaning of his office. Neff Powell, his archdeacon and an old friend, has helped me clarify how diocesan administration works and has guided me through some of the intricacies of the Canons. He and Keith, by reading over the text, have prevented me from making more errors than I thought possible. Lloyd Childers and Henry Craumer, both experienced as senior wardens and leaders in diocesan lay organizations, have also helped me make sure that the book is responsive to the needs of layfolk. Philippa Goodwin, the illustrator of this book, has

6

done a wonderful job of translating often abstract ideas and ancient words into images that speak clearly. To them I am grateful for what is helpful here; I will accept responsibility for what is not.

Raleigh, North Carolina
The Feast of George Herbert
February 27, 1985

A

Abbot: Title of head of a monastic order which lives in an abbey; in the Episcopal Church, the Order of St. Benedict (Benedictines) has an abbey and an abbot in Three Rivers, Michigan, and the Order of the Holy Family has an abbot and an abbey in Denver, Colorado.

Ablutions: Ritual cleansing of the chalice and paten or bread tray after all have received bread and wine during the Eucharist. This is usually performed by the deacon, celebrant, or chalice bearer, and includes consuming bread and wine not received by the congregation, rinsing the paten or bread tray and chalice with water or unconsecrated wine and water, and drying tray and chalice with a purificator. This may take place at the altar, at the credence table, or in the sacristy and may happen at the end of the reception, before the postcommunion prayer, or after the dismissal. An alternative to consuming the consecrated bread and wine is to store them in the aumbry or tabernacle. In any case, the altar is cleared of the eucharistic vessels before the postcommunion prayer.

Absolution: Act whereby a priest or bishop formally pronounces the forgiveness of sins to those who have confessed them, usually making the sign of the cross over the congregation while repeating the words of absolution. A public confession of sins is part of the Daily Offices and the Eucharist on appropriate occasions; private confession is also available (see BCP, 447-52). In some parishes it is part of the ceremonial for members of the congregation to make the sign of the cross on themselves while it is being made over them.

Acclamation: Term for the seasonal versicle and response at the beginning of the Eucharist (BCP, 323, 355) and for the response of the congregation in the middle of some eucharistic prayers. Also known as the salutation.

Figure 1.   Acolyte with Processional Cross

Acolyte: Lay person who assists in worship by performing such functions as carrying the processional cross or crucifix, lighting and extinguishing candles, holding candles at the reading of the Gospel, and helping with the collection of the offering, and the presentation of the bread and wine, usually while wearing an alb or other vestment. Acolytes may be adults or children, but the tradition that young people get their first experience wearing vestments and assisting the priest at the altar by becoming acolytes is a strong one in many parts of the church. [Figure 1]

Action: The "eucharistic action," the ancient fourfold pattern of behavior that is central to the Eucharist regardless of which rite or text is used. Originating in the biblical accounts of Jesus' institution of the Eucharist, the action includes taking (the Offertory), giving thanks (the Eucharistic Prayer), breaking (the Fraction), and distributing (the reception).

Administration, Sentences of: Words said by the celebrant and other servers while distributing bread and wine (see BCP, 338, 365).

Adoration: Generally, any act of worship; more specifically used in the phrase adoration of the blessed sacrament, or benediction, a ritual act of reverence for the consecrated bread of the Eucharist that is part of the worship life of some parishes.

Advent: The first season of the church's liturgical year, beginning on the fourth Sunday before Christmas (Advent Sunday) and running until the first Eucharist of Christmas. Advent is a season of preparation for remembering Christ's incarnation at Christmas and for the fulfillment of his promise to return in power and great glory. This accounts for the emphasis in many of this season's biblical readings on the end time and on God's promises for the people of Israel and the church of Christ. Advent has received renewed emphasis in recent years as the church has sought ways to counter the secularization of Christmas as a cultural holiday characterized by conspicuous consumption. The liturgical color is purple or, in some places, blue.

Advent Calendar: Used to mark the passing of days in the Advent season, Advent calendars usually have a series of doors to open, one for each day in the season. Behind each door is a picture or object leading up to the nativity scene revealed on December 24. Since Advent has not exactly the same number of days each year, commercial Advent calendars usually have 24 doors, one for each day in December before Christmas.

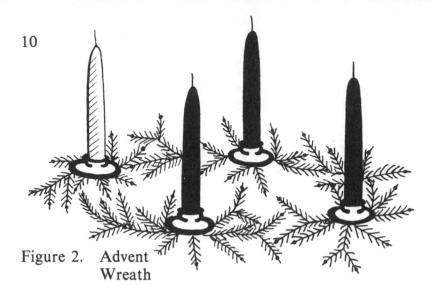

Figure 2.   Advent
Wreath

Advent Wreath: A circle, usually covered with evergreen foliage, with four candle holders. Candle colors may vary: four purple or white, or three purple and one rose or pink. A purple candle is lighted on the First Sunday of Advent and each day thereafter until Christmas. A second purple candle is lighted on the Second Sunday of Advent, and so on until all four candles are lighted on the Fourth Sunday of Advent. If a rose or pink candle is used, it is first lighted on the Third Sunday, reflecting the tradition that the lessons for the Third Sunday are more celebratory than on the other Sundays. A recent development in Advent wreaths is the Christmas candle—usually a larger white candle in the center of the wreath, lit on Christmas Eve midnight services. While large Advent wreaths are used in churches, smaller versions can form the focus of family devotions during the season. [Figure 2]

Agape: Greek word used in the New Testament to mean the love we are called to have for each other as Christians. Paul's famous summary "faith, hope, and love, but the greatest of these is love" (1 Corinthians 13:13) reads *agape* for love. Distinguished in Greek from *eros* (erotic love) and *philia* (fraternal love), *agape* was translated into Latin as *caritas* (as opposed to *cupiditas*) and thus came into English as *charity*. The word actually derives from the experience of early Christians during the eucharistic meal; therefore, we may say that agape is the love we feel for each other as members of the body of Christ, the church.

Agnus Dei: Latin, literally "Lamb of God." The name of the anthem which may be used after the Breaking of Bread in the Eucharist (BCP, 337).

Aisle: Walkway between pews or seats. Churches frequently have a center aisle and one or more side aisles.

Figure 3.   Alb

Alb: White or natural-colored vestment, reaching from the neck to the ankles and often gathered at the waist by a rope or cincture, worn by the celebrant and other ministers at the Eucharist. May be worn together with a detachable collar, or amice, or may come with its collar or hood attached. Worn with a stole and under chasubles, dalmatics, tunicles, and copes, or by itself, depending on the role or order of the wearer. Traditionally made of lightweight material and worn over the cassock, it is now often made of heavier material in a cut that combines features of the cassock and the alb, called a cassock-alb. [Figure 3]

All Saints' Day: November 1; follows All Hallows' Even, or Halloween. Day on which the church remembers the communion of saints, known and unknown, the cloud of witnesses to the faith with which God has surrounded us. This day may also be observed on the Sunday following November 1 and is frequently a major parish celebration.

All Souls' Day: November 2, the day after All Saints', on which all the faithful departed are commemorated.

Alleluia: Hebrew word meaning "praise God," which is used liturgically before and after the proclamation "Christ our Passover is sacrificed for us; Therefore let us keep the feast" (BCP, 337, 364) and on other occasions, but is omitted during Lent.

Alleluia Verse: A text taken from the Bible, combined with the acclamation "Alleluia," which in some places is sung or said before the reading of the Gospel, except in Lent.

Alms: Traditionally money given to the poor, but now generally the money part of the offering, as opposed to the oblations in the phrase *alms and oblations,* which are the bread and wine.

Alms Basin: Plate, basket, or other container passed among the congregation to receive money offerings.

Altar: The table on which the bread and wine are placed during a celebration of the Eucharist. Early altars were free-standing tables; the celebrant faced the congregation across the altar. Later, altars were made out of stone and stood against the east wall of the church building so that the celebrant stood with his back to the congregation. More recently the ancient posture has been recovered so that newer churches again have freestanding altars and some older churches with immovable altars against the east wall are using portable altars. [Plates A and B]

Plate A.   Traditional Altar

14

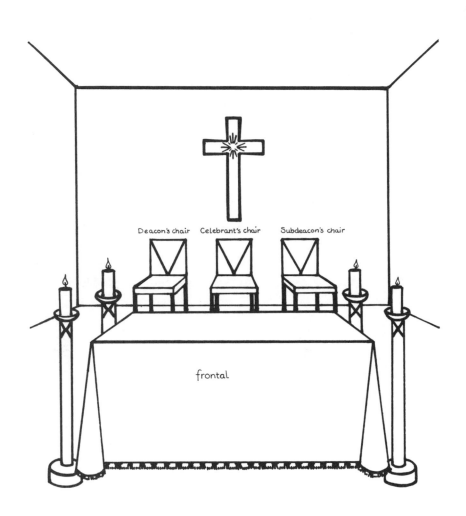

Plate B.   Freestanding Altar

Altar Book: Large book containing texts and music for the celebrant at the Eucharist which is used at the altar.

Altar Cloth: Also called the "fair linen"; a long strip of white linen the width of the altar which covers the top of the altar and hangs down over the ends. It is usually decorated with a cross embroidered in each corner and another embroidered at the middle along one edge.

Altar Cross: Cross or crucifix which hangs above altar or stands on it.

Altar Guild: Parish group organized for the purpose of preparing the altar for celebrations of the Eucharist; work includes making sure that altar hangings are the right color, preparing the chalice, purificators, corporal, and burse, and cleaning up afterwards. Members of the Altar Guild are a valuable resource for the parish, both for the work they do and because they always have the best techniques for getting wine and lipstick stains out of fabric. Since they know where all the hangings, flower containers, and similar church furnishings are stored, they also are the ones who prepare the church for weddings, funerals, readings of the Daily Offices, and other ceremonies.

Altar of Repose: An altar other than the main altar, where in some churches bread and wine consecrated on Maundy Thursday are kept in reserve to be used on Good Friday.

Altar Rail: Railing in front of or to the side of an altar, used to assist those who receive the bread and wine of the Eucharist while kneeling to get up and down, and also to provide them with a place to rest their elbows.

Ambo: Another word for a lectern from which Bible reading and preaching are conducted.

Amen: Hebrew word giving assent or emphasis to what has been said. Used liturgically at the end of prayers and hymns to allow the congregation to give assent (when the prayer is spoken by someone else) or to conclude on a note of affirmation. Making the sign of the cross is a manual act which means the same thing as saying "Amen."

Figure 4.   Amice

Amice: Item of eucharistic dress; a rectangular piece of white or natural cloth worn at the neck with an alb to form a collar or hood. Now often replaced by collar or hood attached to the alb or cassock-alb. [Figure 4]

Anamnesis: From a Greek word meaning "to remember" or "to recall"; refers to the parts of the Great Thanksgiving or Eucharistic Prayer which recount the history of our salvation in a series of God's saving actions in history. When Jesus told his disciples to continue the action with bread and wine, he said, "Do this for the *anamnesis* of me." Usually, the word is understood to mean not just a thinking about again, but a reliving in the present, so that in the Eucharist we do not simply remember Jesus' passion but also participate in its benefits.

Anglican, Anglicanism: England is really "Angleland," or the land of the Angles, one of the Germanic tribes that settled there early in the Christian era; therefore, the Church of England is also *ecclesia anglicana,* or the Anglican Church. Anglicans are properly all those who are communicants of churches—including the Episcopal Church—which are part of the Anglican communion and owe their identity to their historical and liturgical relationship to the Church of England. We usually call ourselves Episcopalians and not Anglicans, although it would be all right to call ourselves Anglicans.

Anglicanism usually refers to the claim of the Church of England to represent a body of Christendom distinct from Orthodox, Roman Catholic, and Protestant traditions. The central concerns of Anglicanism are summarized in the Lambeth Quadrilateral, and suggest that Anglicanism is a tradition that finds its identity in what its members do together, rather than what it insists they affirm. Anglicanism combines Protestant emphasis on the importance of Scripture and individual conscience with Catholic concern for worship, hierarchy, and tradition; it has often been described as a middle way or bridge tradition. While this may be helpful, it obscures the distinctive nature of Anglicanism as a tradition in its own right, complex and hard to pin down but faithful to its desire to share the boundless grace of God.

Anglican Chant: Traditional musical settings for the Psalms and other canticles characterized by chanting the first part of each half-verse on a single note and then using a rhythmic tune for the rest of each half-verse.

Anglican Communion: Worldwide assembly of churches which, in communion with the Church of England, recognize the leadership of the Archbishop of Canterbury. Each member church sends representatives every ten years to the Lambeth Conference to discuss matters of mutual concern. Includes some 64 million members among the Church of England; the Church of Ireland; the Episcopal Church in Scotland; the Church in Wales; our Episcopal Church; the Anglican Church of Canada; the Church of England in Australia; the Episcopal Church of Brazil; the Church in the Province of Burma; the Church of Burundi, Rwanda, and Zaire; the Church of the Province of Central Africa; the Anglican Church in Argentina, Paraguay, and Peru; the Council of Churches in East Asia (including Hong Kong and Macao); the Church in the Province of the Indian Ocean; the Holy Catholic Church in Japan; the Episcopal Church in Jerusalem and the Middle East; the Church of the Province of Kenya; the Church of the Province of Melanesia; the Church of the Province of New Zealand; the Church of the Province of Nigeria; the Church of the Province of Papua, New Guinea; the Church of the Province of Southern Africa; the Church in the Province of Sudan; the Church in the Province of Tanzania; the Church of Uganda; the Church of the Province of West Africa; the Church in the Province of the West Indies; and dioceses in Europe and elsewhere under the jurisdiction of one of the above churches. The local Episcopal parish is thus part of a much larger worldwide body and not an autonomous unit.

Anglican Consultative Council: Representative advisory group made up of bishops, clergy, and lay people selected by the member churches of the Anglican communion which meets every two or three years to provide consultation and guidance for the whole Anglican communion, especially on matters regarding communications, mission, and interchurch relations.

Anointing: Act of applying consecrated oil, used in Baptism, Confirmation, and Ministration to the Sick. Traditionally, an action signifying the gift of the Holy Spirit in such rites, the use of oil is in some places associated with other rites in which the individual so anointed is set apart for special reasons, such as Ordination.

Anthem: English form of the word *antiphon,* usually now referring to musical settings of biblical texts used in the liturgies of the church. The text said or sung at the Breaking of Bread (BCP, 337, 364) is called the Anthem at the Fraction.

Antiphon: Originally a text sung alternately by two choirs; now sentences from Scripture or traditional sources recited before and after the Psalms and canticles in the Daily Offices, the Eucharist, and other services.

Apocrypha: Collection of writings that were part of the Greek Bible of the Jewish community outside of Palestine at the beginning of the Christian era, which became the Bible of Gentile Christians. However, these books were not included in the canon of Scripture established by rabbis in Jerusalem about A.D. 70. Jerome included these books when he translated the Bible into Latin, and the medieval church treated these books as part of authoritative scripture. At the time of the Reformation, however, they came under suspicion in the Reformed traditions. Anglicans use the apocryphal books in liturgical readings and hold them as authoritative "for example of life and instruction of manners" but not for doctrinal matters. A Protestant Bible excludes these books, an Anglican Bible includes them in a special section labeled "The Apocrypha," and a Roman Catholic Bible contains them in the order Jerome found them in the Greek Bible. For a list, see Article VI of the Thirty-Nine Articles of Religion (BCP, 868-69).

Apostles' Creed: Ancient summary statement of the faith which probably derives from baptismal formularies; used in the Prayer Book in the Daily Offices and in the rite for Baptism. It also forms the basis of the text of the Baptismal Covenant and the Renewal of Baptismal Vows (BCP, 292, 304) performed periodically during the year, especially at the Easter Vigil. Along with the Nicene Creed one of the historic statements affirmed by the Lambeth Quadrilateral of 1888 as fundamental to the nature of the church (BCP, 877-78).

Apostolic Succession: The belief that the church today is in direct continuity with the church of the apostles, and is thus part of the "one, holy, catholic, and apostolic church." This continuity is acted out in the rites of ordination and consecration in which bishops, priests, and deacons are ordained by the laying on of hands by a bishop or (in the case of the ordination of a bishop) several bishops of the church, who were in turn ordained by other bishops in what is theoretically an unbroken succession back to the apostles themselves. It is impossible to prove or disprove this continuity; for us, the question of apostolic succession resides more in the office of the bishop, part of whose duty it is to ensure that the faith taught today is the faith of the apostles.

Archbishop: Title given in the Church of England and some other branches of the Anglican communion to bishops who have responsibilities beyond the limits of their dioceses. There are two archbishops in England, the Archbishop of Canterbury and the Archbishop of York, each of whom is responsible for a province containing many dioceses. In addition, the Archbishop of Canterbury is historically regarded as the leader of the entire Church of England and the Anglican communion. In the Episcopal Church, we do not have archbishops and have chosen to call our chief bishop the Presiding Bishop, who, unlike an archbishop, ceases to be a diocesan bishop when elected as Presiding Bishop. The Presiding Bishop's responsibilities are primarily administrative rather than sacramental, although the Presiding Bishop is intended by the Prayer Book to be chief consecrator at the Ordination of bishops.

Archdeacon: Title given to a priest on the administrative staff of a bishop who has primary responsibility for communications with other clergy and who may also have responsibilities for work with small churches, stewardship, and Christian education. An archdeacon's title is The Venerable, and he or she is entitled to wear a purple cassock.

Articles of Religion, Thirty-Nine: The 1563 revision of what were originally forty-two articles written chiefly by Archbishop Cranmer and published in 1553, the Articles of Religion (BCP, 867-76) define the sixteenth-century Anglican position on a wide range of doctrinal, procedural, and practical matters. Although clergy of the Church of England are still required to subscribe to them, they are primarily of historic interest for Episcopalians. If we note places where the Articles were amended for use in our American church after the Revolutionary War, we can understand our history as a church which is in communion with the Church of England, but worshiping in a country where state-supported religion is unconstitutional.

Ascension Day: Day on the liturgical calendar commemorating Christ's ascension and the end of his postresurrection appearances; comes forty days after Easter and always on a Thursday.

Ash Wednesday: Day on the liturgical calendar forty-six days, or forty days other than Sundays, before Easter; marks the beginning of Lent. Follows Mardi Gras, or "Fat Tuesday," or Shrove Tuesday. See special service (BCP,

264-69) which sets an appropriately penitential or preparatory tone for Lent. The name Ash Wednesday derives from the traditional rite of that day in which the celebrant makes the sign of the cross on the foreheads of worshipers, using ashes made from palm leaves left over from the preceding Palm Sunday celebration.

Figure 5.   Aspergillum and Stoup

Aspergillum: A tube with holes at one end and a handle on the other; used to sprinkle holy water on the altar and congregation (an action called the asperges) in parishes where that is part of the traditional ceremonial. Used in connection with a stoup, or holy-water bucket. [Figure 5]

Athanasian Creed: A historic creed of the church, although probably later than the Nicene Creed; takes its name from its traditional (but probably incorrect) attribution to St. Athanasius (see BCP, 864-65). Not one of the two creeds specified by the Lambeth Quadrilateral as essential to the Church.

Aumbry: A recess in or a cupboard on the liturgically east wall of the sanctuary near the altar with a door or other covering, used to store the reserved sacrament and sometimes the chrism, according to the practice of the parish. It has the same function as a tabernacle, but a tabernacle is a storage place for the reserved sacrament located on the altar. In either case, when such a facility is used in church, a sanctuary lamp traditionally hangs over the aumbry or tabernacle; kept burning all the time, this lamp is made to glow red when the aumbry or tabernacle is empty and white when it contains the reserved sacrament.

B

Banns of Marriage: Announces a forthcoming marriage publicly in church. The banns are published on the three Sundays prior to the marriage; for the form used, see BCP, 437. This custom derives from medieval practice intended to insure that those getting married were not closely related to each other and had not made prior commitments to marry others. It now is a delightful way of letting a congregation share in the anticipation of the engaged couple.

Figure 6.   Priest with Baby
at Baptism

Baptism: The sacramental rite of full initiation by water and the Holy Spirit into membership in the Christian church. Baptism has received special emphasis in recent years, a development reflected in its prominent place in the Prayer Book (BCP, 299-311, as well as in the Easter Vigil and Confirmation rites). Baptisms appropriately take place at the main service of the parish at the Easter Vigil, on the Day of Pentecost, All Saints' Day (or the Sunday thereafter), and the First Sunday after Epiphany (the Feast of the Baptism of Jesus). At a Baptism, the congregation renews its own baptismal vows and welcomes the newly baptized into the community. If the person baptized is too young to make the baptismal promises, they are made in the name of the child by parents and godparents. Baptism may be by immersion or by pouring water over the head of the baptized. The Prayer Book strongly urges that Baptisms be done by the bishop when possible, and there is no more powerful action of the church than the Easter Vigil when the bishop baptizes and confirms. But Baptisms may also be done by priests and deacons (or layfolk under special circumstances, see BCP, 312-14). Perhaps the second most powerful image of the church in action is the Sunday morning Baptism in the context of the weekly Eucharist with the children of the parish gathered around to watch, the congregation renewing its own vows, and the child and its parents and godparents standing proudly as the priest baptizes the child. Occasionally, Baptism includes an action in which the newly baptized receives a baptismal candle lit from the Paschal candle or the Gospel candle. [Figure 6]

Baptistry: Traditionally a separate building in which Baptisms occurred; now rarely seen except that something of the old idea is retained in churches where the baptismal font is set apart from the rest of the building in its own space. The virtue of the baptistry is that it provides a distinctive space for the sacrament of Baptism and thus underscores its importance.

Bells: Many churches have bells to call parishioners to worship; in fact, in rural England traditional parish boundaries were marked by how far away a church's bells could be heard. Some parishes also have smaller sets of bells that are rung during the prayer of consecration or Great

Thanksgiving to call the parishioners' attention to special moments; these are called sanctus bells or sacring bells.

Benediction of the Blessed Sacrament: A traditional rite not in the Prayer Book but used in some parishes, often in connection with Evening Prayer, in which a consecrated host is placed on display in a special stand or monstrance and tribute to it is offered in the form of hymns and incense. Generally part of the devotional life of a congregation with special concern for celebrating the real presence of Christ in the Eucharist.

Benedictus Qui Venit: Latin for "Blessed is he who comes," text of an anthem sung or said after the Sanctus in the Eucharist (BCP, 334, 362).

Bible: According to the Lambeth Quadrilateral, Anglicans believe that the "Holy Scriptures of the Old and New Testament" contain "all things necessary to salvation" and are "the rule and ultimate standard of faith." The Prayer Book is biblically centered in that it provides for two cycles of biblical readings, one in the eucharistic lectionary, which includes major portions of the Bible in its three-year cycle of lessons, and one in the Daily Office lectionary, which provides for reading of most of the Bible in its two-year cycle. In general, Episcopalians expect preaching to explore the Scripture lessons appointed for the day rather than the interests or inclinations of the preacher. Only a small number of translations of the Bible are authorized for reading in the church; they include the King James Version of 1611, the Revised Standard Version of 1952, the Jerusalem Bible of 1966, the New English Bible of 1970, the New American Bible of 1970, and the Common Bible (a revision of the Revised Standard Version) of 1973.

Bier: A stand on which the coffin rests in church during the rite of the Burial of the Dead.

Figure 7. Biretta

Biretta: A stiff square hat with three raised corners and a pompom on top sometimes worn by clergy. Priests' birettas are black, while those of bishops are purple. [Figure 7]

Bishop: The chief sacramental officer of the church, and the office which gives our church its name. The Latin word for bishop is *episcopus,* and so the original name of the Episcopal Church said of us that we were the Protestant church with bishops in the United States. Bishops are the chief pastors for their dioceses; they are responsible for ensuring that the faith proclaimed in parishes is the faith of the church. Bishops have the special office to ordain priests and deacons, and together with other bishops to ordain or consecrate other bishops. They are also the chief ministers in the rite of Confirmation, although the Prayer Book encourages bishops to act out their overall pastoral role by performing Baptisms and celebrating the Eucharist when they do Confirmations. Bishops are required to visit all the parishes and missions in their dioceses at regular intervals. They also preside at diocesan conventions and have administrative responsibility for diocesan activities. In the American church there are four kinds of bishops: the Presiding Bishop, the several diocesan bishops, and assisting bishops called coadjutors and suffragans. The Presiding Bishop is the chief administrative officer of the Episcopal Church; he is elected by the House of Bishops, subject to the approval or disapproval of the House of Deputies, for a term ending at the General Convention closest to the Presiding Bishop's sixty-eighth birthday. Each diocese has a diocesan bishop, elected by that diocese meeting in convention to be the chief liturgical and administrative officer of the diocese. A diocesan bishop may be assisted by a bishop coadjutor or a bishop suffragan, also elected by diocesan conventions. A bishop coadjutor is elected to replace the diocesan bishop upon retirement. A bishop suffragan is elected to be an assisting bishop only; a bishop suffragan may succeed a diocesan bishop but has to be elected to that position in addition to being elected bishop suffragan. The traditional insignia of the bishop's office include the bishop's throne (or cathedra) in the cathedral, pastoral staff, miter, pectoral cross, and ring. Bishops may vest in a purple cassock together with a rochet and chimere, or they may wear a white alb together with a cope and mitre. The official title of a bishop is The Right Reverend. [Figure 14]

Bishop's Chaplain: Member of the clergy designated to march before the bishop in procession and carry the bishop's pastoral staff.

Blessed Sacrament: The bread and wine of the Eucharist after the Prayer of Consecration.

Blessing: The pronouncement of God's favor, customarily done by a priest or bishop. Blessings may be of people, as at the end of the Eucharist (BCP, 339, 366), of places, such as homes (BOS, 131-41) and churches (BCP, 567-79), or of things, such as wedding rings (BCP, 427), the water at Baptism (BCP, 306-07), the palms on Passion or Palm Sunday (BCP, 271), or of relationships, such as marriage (BCP, 431). See also blessings of conditions (BOS, 142) such as pregnancy, and of church furnishings (BOS, 177-92), and blessings in homes or over food in special seasons (BOS, 45-48, 93-95).

Blue Boxes: Small distinctive containers used to facilitate the collection of the United Thank Offering; also called mite boxes.

Boat: Small lidded container with a spoon used to carry incense before it is placed in a thurible. [Figure 36]

Book of Common Prayer: The book that makes it possible for the Episcopal Church to be a pragmatic church which understands its identity through participation in corporate worship. The first Book of Common Prayer was produced by Archbishop Thomas Cranmer in 1549; he also produced a revision in 1552. With these books worship could be conducted in English rather than in Latin; they also brought the diverse rites and services of the medieval church together into one book for use by both clergy and layfolk. In 1559, another revision appeared as part of the Elizabethan Settlement of Religion. A later revision, that of 1662, is still the official Prayer Book in the Church of England, although England is now also using a Book of Alternative Services containing modern-language alternatives to most of the official Prayer Book rites. Each church in the Anglican communion has its own adaptation of the Book of Common Prayer. The Prayer Book for Episcopalians has gone through a number of revisions. The first Prayer Book for the American Church was approved in 1789 (BCP, 8); the latest, the Prayer Book of 1979, is now in use. The Prayer Book is essential to the character of the Episcopal Church because its use holds together congregations with very different styles of worship and emphasis within the broader traditions of Christian belief and practice.

Bowing: From very early, Christians have bowed at the mention of Jesus' name (see Philippians 2:10); later, the bow as an act of reverence and honor extended to the altar, the eucharistic elements, and in some places the processional cross as it passes. The development of ceremonial produced a distinction in some parishes between a simple bow (slight inclining of the head and shoulders) for the name of Jesus, and a more pronounced profound bow (bending of the waist) for the altar. Genuflection (kneeling with the body erect until the right knee touches and then standing again) as an act of reverence for the Blessed Sacrament developed from the bow and is part of the tradition of some parishes. [Figures 31-32]

Bread: Bread used in the Eucharist may be either unleavened (usually in the form of individual wafers for communicants and a larger wafer or host for the celebrant) or leavened (often in the form of large single loaves). The emphasis on the action of the community in the Eucharist that characterizes the new Prayer Book has led to more use of loaves of leavened bread, usually baked by parishioners.

Bread Box: Lidded container employed in some places to store and transport unleavened wafers when they are used as bread at the Eucharist. At the Offertory procession, a member of the congregation brings the bread box to the celebrant.

Breviary: A book containing texts to enable the practice of reading the Daily Office. At the time he prepared the first Prayer Book, Cranmer reduced from eight to two the services that marked the monastic day and made them the basis of regular prayer and Bible reading by clergy and layfolk alike; instead of Matins, Lauds, Prime, Terce, Sext, None, Vespers, and Compline, Cranmer's scheme provided Matins (Morning Prayer) and Evensong (Evening Prayer). Anglican Prayer Books have preserved Cranmer's original scheme; the Prayer Book of 1979 also provides texts for offices of Noonday Prayer and Compline, which can be used in addition to Morning and Evening Prayer, and an Order of Worship for Evening that can augment or replace Evening Prayer on occasion. The Church Hymnal Society publishes a Daily Office book and books containing the Daily Office lectionary; together these function as a breviary for Episcopalians.

Bucket: Container for holy water, with a handle. See illustration at **aspergillum.** [Figure 5]

Burial of the Dead: Service found in the Prayer Book in two versions (BCP, 469-505) along with An Order for Burial (BCP, 506-07), which provides an outline of a burial rite for use when neither of the regular forms is deemed appropriate. The burial rites assume that they will take place in the context of a celebration of the Eucharist. Episcopal funerals are closed-casket services, and the coffin is to be covered by a simple drape, or pall, rather than flowers. Each parish should have a pall; the point is that in death we are all equal, not distinguishable by the size of the display of flowers we are able to command in our memory. The Prayer Book also contains a rite for the Committal at the grave, including the traditional casting of earth upon the coffin. Episcopal funerals are Easter liturgies which take their meaning from the hope of resurrection. The liturgical color is white.

Burse: An envelope or pocket of two square pieces of stiff material covered with cloth in one of the liturgical colors; made so that it can contain folded cloths, specifically the corporal or white linen cloth placed on the altar at the time of setting up for the Eucharist and the purificators used to wipe the chalice during the administration of the wine. The burse is used in connection with a veil of the same material to cover the chalice as it is brought to the altar when that is part of the ceremonial style of the parish. The burse may also be decorated with an embroidered cross or other symbol. See illustration at **paten.** [Figure 26]

C

Calendar: The calendar of the church year (sometimes spelled kalendar) has six seasons: Advent, Christmas, Epiphany, Lent, Easter, and Pentecost. It is structured in relationship to the two major Feasts of Christmas and Easter (BCP, 15-18). The Advent season begins with the First Sunday of Advent (four Sundays before Christmas). The Christmas season runs twelve days from December 25 to January 5 and is followed by the Feast of the Epiphany (January 6) and the Epiphany season, which runs until Ash Wednesday, forty weekdays and six Sundays before Easter. The date of Easter, the first Sunday on or after the full moon after the vernal equinox (March 21), because it moves between March 23 and April 25, determines the length of the Epiphany season as well as the Pentecost season, which begins with the Feast of Pentecost, fifty days after Easter. The Pentecost season then extends for a variable number of Sundays until the year begins again with the First Sunday of Advent. The liturgical calendar also co-exists with the calendar of the saints (BCP, 19-33), a series of days for commemorating notable figures from the church's past. Since each saint on the calendar of the saints has the same day each year, there are times in which a saint's day conflicts with a Sunday or other major feast day from the seasonal calendar. When that happens, the saint's day is moved to the nearest available open day after the official day.

Candidate: A candidate for Holy Orders is usually in his or her second or third year of formal theological study in a seminary or other educational situation. He or she is appointed a candidate by the bishop of the postulant's diocese, usually upon the recommendation of the diocesan Commission on Ministry and with the consent of the Standing Committee after interviews, physical and psychiatric exams, and recommendations from the aspirant's home parish vestry, from his or her rector, and from the seminary being attended. Candidates have been postulants usually for a year or more before advancing to candidacy. Usually all that stands between a candidate for Holy Orders and ordination is successful completion of a theological education, performing satisfactorally on the General Ordination Exams, and passing a final review by the Commission on Ministry, the Standing Committee, and the bishop.

Candles: Used in the Episcopal Church for a wide variety of symbolic and functional purposes, candles enrich our ceremonial life. Two may be placed on the altar; these are sometimes referred to as the Epistle candle and the Gospel candle because of an old tradition of starting with the service book or altar missal on the side of the altar to the celebrant's right and then moving it to the other side before the reading of the Gospel. As part of this tradition, the Gospel candle was lit first and extinguished last. Other candles may be placed behind the altar on the reredos (if the church is arranged traditionally) or on stands at the corners of the altar (if the church is arranged with a freestanding altar). Candles may also be carried in procession or held near the Gospel when it is read; they are then called processional torches. The Paschal candle, a special candle frequently decorated with a cross and/or other symbols, is the first thing to be lighted from the new fire at the Easter Vigil. A baptismal candle, lit from the Paschal candle during the Easter season but from the Gospel candle at other times, may be presented to the newly baptized. Candles are also used in the Advent wreath and may be carried by the entire congregation at the Easter Vigil and at Candlemas. They are also important parts of the imagery of Epiphany. In a parish where there are statues of the saints, banks of candles, called votive lights, are lighted by those who offer prayer before the statues. The carrying, lighting, and extinguishing of candles are important parts of the duties of acolytes.

Candlemas: The feast also known as the Presentation of Our Lord Jesus Christ in the Temple, or the Purification of the Blessed Virgin Mary, observed on February 2. The name comes from the tradition of blessing candles at this feast and carrying them in procession; extensive use of candles in procession and to light the church is still characteristic of the ceremonial for this day.

Canon: A Greek word that came to mean a unit by which things are measured. Thus we speak of the canon of Scripture as the list of books regarded as having authority for the church, canon law as the list of rules by which the church is guided and governed, and the canon of the Mass as the prayer of consecration or Great Thanksgiving which summarizes the history of salvation and places the community gathered at the altar within it.

Canon Law: The national Episcopal Church and each diocese of the church have ecclesiastical laws which set forth the rules and procedures by which the church and its members are to live. These are sometimes referred to merely as the Canons of the Church. Copies of canon law are available to anyone. Diocesan canons must conform to the national canons; canons can be changed only by a vote of a diocese or the national church meeting in convention. Canons outline procedures such as the steps required before someone is married or ordained or elected bishop.

Canon of Scripture: The list of books accepted as having the authority of Scripture. This list was not arrived at all at once but developed over time; this process included both the addition and deletion of books. The canon of the Old Testament existed in two forms, that of Greek-speaking Jews living outside of Palestine and that of the Jewish community still living near Jerusalem early in the Christian era. The canon of the New Testament was fixed in its present form by the end of the fourth century A.D. At the Reformation, Protestant churches accepted the Old Testament canon of the Jerusalem community, while Roman Catholics retained the medieval canon, which was that of Greek-speaking Jews. Anglicans retained the books excluded from the medieval Bible by Protestants but grouped them in a special section called the Apocrypha; these are read in church and are held as authoritative for moral instruction but not for doctrinal judgment.

Canon of the Eucharist, or Mass: The prayer over the elements which begins with the Sursum Corda, or "Lift up your hearts." Includes among its elements (in some versions) a seasonal or occasional preface, a section of *anamnesis* or remembering of the story of salvation (what God has done), a recitation of the words of institution (what Jesus did and commanded us to continue), an *epiklesis* or invocation of the Holy Spirit on the gifts and on us (what we want God to do now), and a proclamation of Jesus' lordship and his place in the Trinity, all leading up to a great, resounding "Amen" by the whole congregation. The word *Eucharist* means "thanksgiving," and so the Eucharistic Prayer or canon is also The Great Thanksgiving (BCP, 333-36, 340-43, 361-63, 367-75; see also the special forms on 402-05).

Canon of a Cathedral: One who is on the staff of a cathedral, and is thus on its official or canonical roster. Cathedral canons form a staff for the work of the bishop in the diocese, and also for the pastoral work of the cathedral itself.

Canonical Residence: Every priest and deacon is "canonically resident" in a particular diocese and responsible to the bishop of that diocese. Only in that diocese is she or he licensed to function sacramentally; in other dioceses, the permission of the bishop must be obtained. It is possible to change canonical residence, but the bishop of the diocese in which one is canonically resident must write a letter dimissory to the bishop of the new diocese, who must accept it for the change of canonical residence to take place.

Canonization: Traditionally the process by which someone is proclaimed a saint. In the Roman Catholic Church, this process is a lengthy and drawn-out procedure which has nevertheless resulted in a Roman Catholic calendar of saints which is practically full. The Church of England at the Reformation radically reduced the number of saints on the Anglican calendar, essentially to New Testament figures, and has been very reluctant to get into the business of choosing new ones. The Episcopal Church has recently added to the calendar a number of figures from the medieval, Reformation, and modern periods; see BCP, 19-30 for the full list. For a name to be included in the Episcopal calendar of the saints, the Standing Liturgical Commission must recommend it to the General Convention of the church, which then accepts or rejects the recommendation. To Roman Catholics, a saint is a figure whom one can ask to intercede with God on one's behalf; to Episcopalians, a saint is a witness to the faith and an example to follow.

Canterbury: City in England on site of the first church established by St. Augustine when he came to Christianize England in A.D. 597; the see city of the province of Canterbury and site of the cathedral of the Archbishop of Canterbury, primate of all England and the spiritual leader of the Anglican communion.

Canterbury Cap: A square cap, always in black, made of soft material and worn by some clergy. Paintings of Thomas Cranmer and other clergy of the Reformation period show them wearing Canterbury caps. [Figure 8]

Figure 8.   Canterbury Cap

Canterbury, Archbishop of: Bishop of the archepiscopal see of Canterbury and legally the head of the Church of England, the Archbishop of Canterbury is the spiritual head of the Anglican communion, although he has no legal authority in any branch of the Anglican communion except the Church of England. The Archbishop of Canterbury also has a London residence on the south bank of the Thames River, at Lambeth Palace.

Canticle: A song based on biblical texts or incorporating biblical texts in a nonbiblical context (e.g., Te Deum Laudamus) other than the psalms; used regularly in the liturgical worship of the church, especially after the lessons at Morning or Evening Prayer, or as the Song of Praise in the Eucharist. Examples include the Magnificat (BCP, 65, 119) and the Nunc Dimittis (BCP, 66, 120).

Cantor: Person, ordained or lay, who has special gifts for singing and uses them to enrich the worship of the church by leading a long sung text, such as the Great Litany, the Exsultet, or the parts of the passion Gospels.

Cappa Nigra: A black cloak, usually made of wool, with a hood, worn outdoors by some clergy. Frequently worn over vestments at the end of services when clergy are greeting parishioners at the door of the church building in cold weather.

Figure 9. Cassock

Cassock: A long neck-to-ankle vestment which is the basic item of clerical attire. Priests usually wear black cassocks, while bishops and archdeacons wear purple. The cassock was once ordinary street clothing for clergy, and all other vestments, including albs and surplices, went on top of the cassock. Now, with the development of cassock-albs and albs of heavy material, clergy wear cassocks with surplices for the offices and for taking part in Eucharists when they are not among the chief ministers. There are two basic styles of cassocks: (1) the Anglican cassock, which is double-breasted and fastens only at the shoulders, and (2) the Roman cassock, which is single-breasted and buttons all the way down the front. Both are usually worn with a sash or cincture at the waist; occasionally a short cape may be worn with a cassock. [Figure 9]

Cassock-alb: A vestment that combines the color of the alb (white or natural) with the cut and material of the Anglican cassock. The cassock-alb may thus be worn under a chasuble at the Eucharist without a cassock under it. Cassock-albs come with either a high collar or a hood at the neck to take the place of the amice. [Figure 3]

Catechism: Originally the name given to prebaptismal instructions for children and adults, the word came to mean the book containing those instructions, usually put in the form of questions and answers. The Prayer Book contains the current Episcopal catechism on pp. 843-62 under the title An Outline of the Faith.

Catechist: Specifically, one who teaches the catechism; more generally, one responsible for basic instruction in the Christian faith.

Catechizing: Teaching the catechism; sometimes used to refer to instruction in the basics of the Christian faith whether or not it follows the question-and-answer form traditional in catechisms and catechizing.

Catechumens: In the early church, those preparing during Lent for baptism at the Easter Vigil. In recent years, with the renewed emphasis on the Easter Vigil as the central Eucharist of the Christian year and with an increase in the number of adult baptisms, the idea of a catecumenate has been recovered in some places. The Book of Occasional Services contains rites for forming baptismal candidates into a catecumenate, along with their sponsors, for a period of formal preparation during Lent or some other period before a day for baptisms (BOS, 112-25).

Cathedral: One sign of the office of a bishop is his throne, or cathedra; the church which houses the bishop's cathedra is his cathedral. Traditionally each diocese has a cathedral, which differs from a parish church in that it does not have a formal congregation, although it may have regular worshipers. The cathedral has a staff of clergy headed by a dean; clergy on the dean's staff are called canons. Today a number of dioceses do not have cathedrals but provide offices for the bishop and staff in a diocesan house. Some large dioceses may have both. Cathedrals traditionally have rich liturgical lives augmented by splendid music; to provide choristers, a number of cathedrals have schools attached to them. Among the best known Episcopal cathedrals are the Cathedral of St. John the Divine in New York City, the Cathedral of Saint Peter and Saint Paul in Washington, D.C. (also known as the National Cathedral), and Grace Cathedral in San Francisco.

Catholic: A word meaning "general" or "universal" which has come to have a number of meanings in the church. It is used to distinguish the church universal from local congregations, to mean "orthodox" instead of "heretical," to recall the undivided church before the divisions which separated the Eastern from the Western churches in 1054, to name churches which claim an unbroken continuity of faith and tradition from the age of the apostles (including Roman Catholic, Anglican, and Orthodox traditions), and to mean those who value continuity and unity. Traditionally, the "catholic" part of the creedal phrase "one holy catholic and apostolic church" refers to the claim that what the church believes, it has always and everywhere believed.

Plate C.

Traditional
Church
Floor Plan

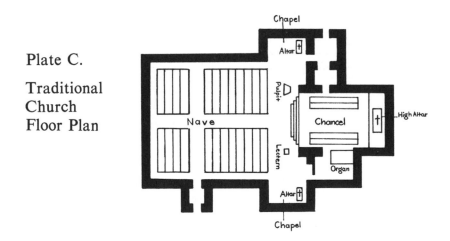

Celebrant: The bishop or priest who officiates at the altar during a celebration of the Eucharist, as opposed to any assisting clergy. On some occasions, such as the Eucharist at a diocesan convention, the celebrant may be joined by other priests who say at least part of the Prayer of Consecration together, becoming concelebrants engaging in a concelebration of the Eucharist. The bishop is, appropriately, the celebrant when present; there is a real sense in which a priest functioning as the celebrant is there in place of the bishop.

Celebrant's Chair: The seat occupied by the celebrant at the Eucharist; with a traditional altar against the east wall, the celebrant's chair, or sedilia, is against the wall to the congregation's right, but with a freestanding altar the celebrant's chair is appropriately behind the altar facing the west wall of the church building.

Censer: A thurible, or incense pot. [Figure 36]

Plate D.
Modern Church
Floor Plan

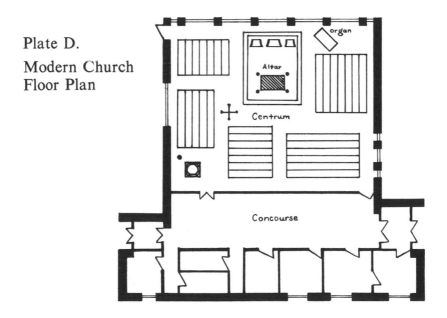

Centrum: Name given by some contemporary church architects to the room where the Eucharist is usually celebrated. Traditional churches are divided into two spaces, a nave (where the people sit) and a choir (where the clergy, choir, and servers sit and where the altar is). Modern churches combine the functions of nave and choir in a single room where all participants become part of a single community engaged in a single action together at the altar. This room, neither nave nor choir, has been given the name centrum. [Plate D]

Ceremonial: Term for how the rites of the church are done, including what people wear, what they do and where, and how they interact with each other. Liturgics usually refers to the study of the words of the rites; ceremonial refers to what is done as those words are spoken.

Figure 10.   Chalice with Purificator

Chalice: The cup used to contain the wine consecrated during the Eucharist. Chalices are traditionally made of silver, but contemporary chalices are often made of pewter or ceramic. Good ones contain enough wine to permit a large number of people to receive the wine between refills and are shaped so as to discourage spilling. Some chalices have a knob underneath the bowl for easy gripping. Chalices may be brought to the altar open, covered by a purificator, or as part of a full "stack" with a purificator, a paten or bread tray, a pall or stiff square of cloth used to support the veil over the chalice, a veil, and a burse. [Figure 26]

Chalice Bearer: Layperson licensed by the bishop of a diocese to administer the chalice at the Eucharist, usually after a period of study and training. Lay chalice bearers can function as subdeacons or servers; they usually vest in an alb and cincture, and may wear a tunicle if the deacon wears a dalmatic. Lay chalice bearers may also be layreaders and may read the epistle in the Eucharist.

Chalice Veil: A square cloth, of the same material and color as the vestments, which is used, together with the pall and burse, to cover the chalice and paten when they are not in use. The burse rides on top of the chalice veil. The chalice veil, with the vestments, is changed as the liturgical colors change. [Figure 10]

Chancel: In a traditional church, the area around the altar, including in some arrangements the whole choir area east of the nave; thus the term "chancel choir." [Plate C]

Chancel Screen: A screen dividing the chancel from the nave; also called a rood screen. Now rarely seen, except that such screens often had on top a cross (or rood) with Jesus as king, flanked by statues of two saints in adoring poses; even where the screen has been taken down to enable the congregation to see what is going on in the chancel, the rood itself often remains.

Chant: A manner of singing Psalms, canticles, and other parts of the liturgy. The best-known versions are Gregorian chant (plainsong) and Anglican chant.

Chapel: (1) The place of worship in a private institution such as a school, seminary, or hospital; (2) part of a large church where an altar is placed separate from the main altar of the church. Such a side chapel is often dedicated to a specific saint, especially the Blessed Virgin Mary (Our Lady, thus they are known as "Lady Chapels"). [Plate C]

Chaplain: A priest with special, often institutional, responsibilities outside of a parish. Clergy who minister to patients in hospitals, students and faculty at a school or college, or the military are called chaplains.

Chapter: The collective membership of a corporate body responsible for an ecclesiastical institution such as a cathedral or a religious house.

Figure 11. Chasuble

Chasuble: Outermost garment worn over an alb and stole by priests and bishops when celebrating the Eucharist. The chasuble is usually oval-shaped with an opening in the center for the celebrant's head and slips over the head like a poncho so that it drapes over the arms, chest, and back. Some chasubles are cut very full so that they have to be folded back over the celebrant's arms. The chasuble can be made in a variety of materials in the liturgical colors and can be decorated with stripes of contrasting color (called orphreys) or liturgical symbols. A chasuble can be worn by the celebrant when there are assisting ministers in albs and stoles, but a full eucharistic set of vestments includes a dalmatic for the deacon and a tunicle for the lay chalice bearer designed to match the chasuble. Frequently, chasubles and stoles have been designed and made by parish members as a gesture of love and support for clergy and of lay participation in the liturgical life of the church. [Figure 11]

Chimere: Red or black sleeveless, long vest-like gown, usually of silk or satin, worn by Episcopal bishops over a white rochet and a purple or black cassock. See illustration at **rochet.** [Figure 30]

Choir: An organized group of singers who contribute to the celebration of the church's liturgies. They may function primarily to support congregational singing, or they may offer special music of their own. Also, in a traditional church building, the choir usually sits in the chancel, so the chancel is also called the choir of the church. But choirs may also sit in other places in the church building, especially in contemporary designs where the chancel and the nave are not distinguished from each other. [Plate C]

Chrism: Either olive oil or a mixture of olive oil and balsam, consecrated by a bishop, which may be used in Baptism (BCP, 308), Confirmation, and Ordinations. To be distinguished from the oil of unction, which may be blessed by a priest or bishop and which is used in Ministration to the Sick (BCP, 453-61). In some dioceses, the clergy gather with their bishop for a special Eucharist on Maundy Thursday, at which oil is consecrated for all parishes at one time.

Chrismation: Act of anointing someone with the oil of chrism.

Christ the King, Feast of: Some places observe the Last Sunday after Pentecost as a feast celebrating the authority of Christ over all creation; it is called the Feast of Christ the King.

Christen: Another word for "to baptize." Since the giving of a name is part of baptism, *to christen* has also come to mean "to give a name to" or "to use for the first time"; thus we also christen ships and the like.

Christmas: December 25, the Feast of the Nativity of Christ, and the following eleven days until January 6, the Feast of the Epiphany. Christmas Day is usually begun officially with a Eucharist at midnight on Christmas Eve and continues with additional services on Christmas morning.

Church Army: Voluntary organization of Anglican layfolk founded in England in 1882 on the model of the Salvation Army by The Rev. Wilson Carlile. The Church Army encourages and supports lay people to pursue ministries to which they have been called and empowered by the Holy Spirit and commissions them as officers in the Church Army. The address of the American headquarters can be found in the Episcopal Church Annual.

Church Year: The church year (BCP, 15-18) has six seasons: Advent, Christmas, Epiphany, Lent, Easter, and Pentecost. It is structured in relationship to the two major feasts of Christmas (with its fixed date) and Easter (with its movable date). The Advent season begins with the First Sunday of Advent (four Sundays before Christmas). The Christmas season runs twelve days from December 25 to January 6, the Feast of the Epiphany, and is followed by the Epiphany season, which runs until Ash Wednesday, forty weekdays and six Sundays before Easter. The date of Easter, which is the first Sunday on or after the full moon after the vernal equinox (March 21), because it moves between March 23 and April 25, determines the length of the Epiphany season as well as the Pentecost season, which begins with the Feast of Pentecost, fifty days after Easter. The Pentecost season then extends for a variable number of Sundays until the year begins again with the First Sunday of Advent.

Church of England: The Church of England is distinguishable from the church *in* England in that before the 1530s the church in England was part of western Christendom. During the reign of Henry VIII, as a result of the controversy over his divorce from Catherine of Aragon, the church was separated from allegiance to the papacy and became independent although otherwise unchanged. With time and especially during the reign of Edward VI (1547-1553) the now-independent Church of England went through a reformation that produced the English Bible and the Book of Common Prayer. It is therefore proper to say that the Church of England represents both a continuity with the earliest days of the Christian era and a church affected deeply by the Reformation. As a result of the spread of British colonies around the world, together with Anglican missionary efforts, the Church of England eventually created a worldwide association of independent churches totaling over 64 million members called the Anglican communion. Each of these independent churches owes the origins of its identity and worship to the Church of England and retains a sense of regard for the Archbishop of Canterbury as its spiritual leader.

Ciborium: A chalice-shaped vessel with a lid for holding and transporting wafers when they are used for eucharistic bread. The ciborium is used as a container for the consecrated bread in a tabernacle or aumbry, when keeping the reserved sacrament on hand is part of the tradition of a parish. It may also be used as a bread box containing unconsecrated wafers brought forward at the Offertory and presented to the celebrant by a member of the congregation. Ciboria often come with matching chalices in sets.

Cincture: A rope or sash in a color to match the cassock or alb which it binds at the waist. Usually the cincture is tied with a simple slip knot on the left side and allowed to hang, but the celebrant knots his or her cincture in the middle and forms a loop on either side of the knot, creating an opening

48

through which the ends of a stole pass to secure the stole so that it will not flap around during the actions taken by the celebrant during the Eucharist. The cincture may have knots or tassels at the ends; it is also called a girdle.

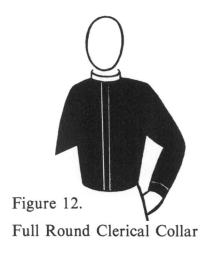

Figure 12.
Full Round Clerical Collar

Figure 13.   Tab Collar

Clerical Collar: A white detachable collar worn with a black shirt to indicate that the wearer is an ordained person. Variations include the tab-collared shirt, which has an attached, matching neck band and a white tab that is inserted in the front, and the rabat vest, in which a black front with a white attached collar is worn over a white collarless shirt. Although the detachable collar was standard equipment for our ancestors, clergy are perhaps the only people who still need collar buttons, used to attach the clerical collar. Clergy shirts are also available in a variety of colors other than black; bishops wear purple clergy shirts with their white collars. [Figures 12 and 13]

Clerical Order: Delegates to a diocesan convention make up two orders, the clerical and the lay. Votes are taken in each order separately, and a majority of votes in both orders is required to pass a measure. The clerical order as a group also exists in the House of Deputies at General Conventions, at which a similar division of votes occurs.

Clericals: Distinctive clerical street attire, as distinct from vestments, which are worn only in the conduct of worship. *Clericals* traditionally referred to the black suit worn by some clergy, but may also refer simply to the clergy shirt. Really means clothing that would readily identify the wearer as an ordained person. When two ordained persons are going somewhere and style of dress is not dictated, one may ask the other, "Are you going to wear clericals?"

Clericus: An informal local association of clergy for mutual support and sharing of concerns.

Cloak: Long black outer garment with a deep collar, usually of wool, which fastens at the breast with a chain and clasp. Worn outdoors by clergy, often over vestments on cold days when greeting parishioners at the door of the church building.

Cloister: Literally a covered walkway with an open colonnade on one side that runs around a courtyard or between two buildings; because cloisters were often part of a monastery or convent, the word came to mean the place where monks or nuns lived. Religious orders which do not permit their members to leave the monastery or convent are called cloistered orders.

Coadjutor, Bishop: A bishop elected by a diocesan convention to become the bishop of that diocese upon the retirement or resignation of the current diocesan bishop. Distinct from a suffragan bishop in that a bishop coadjutor is elected to become diocesan bishop, while a suffragan bishop is elected only to assist the diocesan bishop.

Collect: A short prayer containing an invocation, a petition, and a claiming of the right to appeal in Christ's name or an ascription of glory to God. For Episcopalians, the word is usually thought of as referring to the variable prayer which is called the Collect for the Day and which immediately precedes the reading of the lessons, although a collect or collect-like prayer can appear at other places in the worship of the church. See for example the Solemn Collects in the Good Friday service (BCP, 277-80). The name suggests that a number of themes or concerns have been "collected" in such prayers.

Colors, Liturgical: The colors of vestments, altar cloths, and other church decorations which are changed to mark different seasons or occasions. In general, the color of Advent is purple; Christmas is white; Epiphany is white, changing to green after the First Sunday; Lent is purple or natural linen; Holy Week is red; Easter is white; and Pentecost is red on the day and green thereafter, except Trinity Sunday, which is white. In addition, the color is white for weddings and funerals; white for the saints' days, or red if the saint is also a martyr; red for ordinations. In some places, Advent is blue; requiems may be purple or black. One is advised to consult a liturgical calendar and local custom for the finer points here.

Columbarium: A space reserved in a wall of a church building or its grounds where the ashes of dead church members can be placed and noted with a marker. Traditionally graveyards were adjacent to church buildings, but this practice is less and less possible today. The columbarium makes it possible for people's remains to be in or near their parish churches, reminding us of the communion of the saints, both living and dead.

Comfortable Words: In the Rite One Eucharist the priest has the option of proclaiming "the Word of God to all who truly turn to him" (BCP, 332). In earlier versions of the Prayer Book, the priest said that these were "comfortable words our Savior Christ sayeth unto all who truly turn to him"; thus the sentences of scripture given here are called the comfortable words.

Committal: In the funeral rites, the text used at the grave-side (BCP, 484-87, 501-03), including the ritual casting of earth on the coffin.

Communicant: A *communicant* of the Episcopal Church is a member who has received Holy Communion in the church at least three times in the past year. An *adult communicant* is someone who meets the basic requirement and who is also sixteen years of age or older. A *communicant in good standing* is one who has received Holy Communion at least three times ("unless for good cause prevented") and who has also been "faithful in working, praying, and giving for the spread of the Kingdom of God." One must be a communicant in good standing to be eligible for election to the vestry or mission committee. All parishes and missions are required to keep rosters of their members and communicants. See **member.**

Communicate, To: Verb used to mean either to administer communion to someone, or to receive communion from someone.

Communion of Saints: The doctrine that a spiritual union exists between Christ and all Christians living or dead; *saint* here is used in its original sense as meaning any baptized Christian.

Companion Diocese: Many dioceses in the Episcopal Church have formed official relationships with other dioceses in the Anglican communion, for mutual support. These are said to be companion dioceses. Clergy and layfolk from one may visit the other and engage in joint programs; part of the purpose is to remind us that we are members of a worldwide church and to help us understand what different branches have in common as well as how and why we are different.

Compline: The last of the traditional monastic offices, Compline was said just before bedtime. Cranmer, in 1549, consolidated Compline and other afternoon offices into Evensong. The Prayer Book of 1979 restores Compline as a late evening office (BCP, 127-35) to be used in addition to Evensong or by itself.

Concelebration: The joint celebration of the Eucharist by a number of bishops or priests who say at least part of the canon together, concelebration is especially impressive at a Eucharist when the bishop is joined at the altar by a group of clergy. It is an ancient practice which has recently been revived. Those who celebrate with the principal celebrant are called concelebrants.

Concourse: Name given by some modern church architects to a space that takes over the entrance function of the old narthex but is deliberately much bigger to provide a place where the congregation can gather and enjoy community before or after the Eucharist or at other times. [Plate D]

Confession, General and Private: Archbishop Cranmer set the tone for Anglicans when he abolished the medieval requirement of private confession and absolution before one could receive the Eucharist and provided for public confession and absolution at both Morning and Evening Prayer and at the Eucharist. Cranmer's goal was to encourage more frequent communions than was medieval practice, when people required by law to receive the Eucharist even as infrequently as two or three times a year were still reluctant to participate. Private confession was never abolished in Anglican churches, however, and the Prayer Book provides two different versions of the rite (BCP, 447-52), calling both the Reconciliation of a Penitent. In some parts of the church, private confession is a regular and accepted part of parish life; in others, it is not. Where it is, the General Confession may be thought of as dealing with the shortcomings of the church as a community; private confession, with those of individuals. Where private confession is available for those who seek it but is not a part of everyday parish life, the General Confession is the vehicle for confessing sin both of the community and of the individual. Things told a priest under the seal of the confessional may not be revealed by the priest to others.

Confessional: A small booth or room set aside for the hearing of private confessions, usually found near the entrance to the church building.

Confirmation: A rite in which we express faith and commitment to Christ and, by prayer and the laying on of hands by a bishop, receive strength from the Holy Spirit to continue in the life of faith and commitment. Confirmation is prepared for through a period of study in confirmation class or enquirers' class and involves the reaffirmation of baptismal vows (see BCP, 413-19). The acceptance of adult responsibility in the church may be repeated; the service is then called one of Reaffirmation (BCP, 419). Adults baptized by a priest are expected to be confirmed also, but adults baptized by a bishop with the laying on of hands may consider themselves confirmed as well (BCP, 412). The service of Reaffirmation is still available, however. When someone confirmed in the Roman Catholic Church or one of the Orthodox churches goes through this service as a way of identifying publicly with the Episcopal Church, the rite is said to be one of reception (BCP, 418).

Confirmation Class: Group preparing for Confirmation under the direction of the rector or other designated person; also known as an enquirers' class.

Consecration: In the Eucharist, the action by which the bread and wine become for us the body and blood of Christ. This includes the offering of the elements, the giving of thanks (the canon, or Great Thanksgiving), the breaking of the bread, and the giving of the bread and wine. This action is of the whole community gathered for the Eucharist; it is not just an action of the celebrant. *Consecration* is also sometimes used to describe the rite for the ordination of a bishop or the rites by which altars, chalices, patens, and church buildings are set apart for the service of God.

Constitution: Set of directions specifying how the church is to be organized and governed. There is one Constitution for the national church; each diocese also has a constitution, which adapts the national Constitution for diocesan use. The Constitution spells out the composition of a convention, its required officers, and the qualifications for delegates, among other things. Usually the Constitution is bound together with the Canons. The vote of a single convention is all that is required to change or amend the Canons, but the vote of two consecutive conventions is required to change or amend the Constitution.

Consultant: A professional, ordained or lay, whose job is to help congregations make good decisions at critical times in the life of a parish, such as times of internal conflict or major decision-making. Consultants have special training in helping groups with difficult processes, such as deciding whether to expand facilities, choosing a new rector, training a new vestry, or introducing a new Sunday school curriculum. Usually a diocesan headquarters has a list of consultants who have proved to be effective in the past and will share that list with a parish. A bishop may also require a parish to work with a consultant before it calls a new rector.

Convent: The building in which a group of nuns lives, or the group itself.

Convert: Someone who is not a "cradle Episcopalian," who did not start life as an Episcopalian but became one along the way. Converts are in good company in the Episcopal Church; at one time, for example, rumor had it that over half of Episcopal clergy were converts.

Figure 14. Bishop
in Cope and Mitre
with Pastoral Staff

Cope: A semicircular cloak made in materials and liturgical colors to match other vestments or liturgical hangings in use. The cope may be worn over an alb and stole by the celebrant in procession to the altar and during the early part of the Eucharist; he or she may change into a chasuble at the Offertory or keep the cope on throughout the Eucharist. Wearing a cope while celebrating the Eucharist in cathedrals was standard practice in England from the middle of the sixteenth century. Bishops often wear copes and mitres when they function liturgically, especially for confirmations and in processions. [Figure 14]

Corporal: A large square of white linen which is carried to the altar in the burse and is spread on the altar at the beginning of the process of preparing the altar at the Offertory. The bread and chalice are placed on the corporal during the prayer of consecration.

Cotta: A white vestment similar to a surplice but shorter and less fully cut, worn over cassocks in some places by choirs and acolytes and by assisting clergy.

Credence Table: Traditionally, a small table or shelf found near the altar which holds the chalice and other accessories needed at the Offertory for preparing the altar to receive the bread and wine in procession. In contemporary church architecture, the credence table is often placed near the entrance to the room where the Eucharist is celebrated; the Offertory procession begins at this location.

Creed: A concise, formal, authorized statement of the faith of the church; the word comes from the Latin *credo*, meaning "I believe." The two most important creeds are the Apostles' Creed (BCP, 53) and the Nicene Creed (BCP, 358).

Creche: The nativity scene with Mary, Joseph, the baby Jesus in a manger, and perhaps other figures. In some parishes it is traditional to set up such a scene at Christmas; the Book of Occasional Services provides a rite in which the procession into church pauses at the creche for a moment, there is a versicle and response, and a collect is read (BOS, 34-5).

Cremation: The burning of the body of a deceased person, a practice approved by the Episcopal Church. See **columbarium.**

Crosier: One of the signs of the office of a bishop; a staff, often in the shape of a shepherd's crook, carried by the bishop or the bishop's chaplain in procession and held by the bishop when pronouncing an episcopal blessing.

Cross: A major symbol in Episcopal churches. The traditional Gothic architectural style for church buildings is in the shape of a cross, with the choir and nave forming the vertical axis of the cross and the transepts forming the horizontal axis. [Plate C] Many Episcopal churches have a cross on the altar; others have large crosses hanging prominently on the wall above or behind the altar. Processional crosses are also carried at the head of processions of acolytes, choristers, lay chalice bearers, and clergy. Crosses are also prominently displayed outside on the tops of Episcopal

churches; small ones are worn by clergy, acolytes, and anyone else who wants to. See also **sign of the cross.**

Figure 15.   Celebrant
Making Sign of Cross
in Blessing

Crucifer: Person who carries a cross or crucifix at the head
of an ecclesiastical procession.

Figure 16.   Crucifix

Crucifix: A cross bearing the figure of Jesus with arms
outstretched. There are two forms: (1) depicting the cruci-
fied Jesus with his arms and feet nailed to the cross and a
crown of thorns on his head [Figure 16]; (2) depicting
Christ triumphant, the risen Christ, a splendid crown on his
head, wearing eucharistic vestments. In this latter form the

cross and the resurrection are combined into one symbol, called the Christus Rex, or Christ the King.

Cruet: The vessel in which wine or water is brought to the altar; usually made of silver, glass, or pottery, with a stopper.

Crypt: The basement or vault beneath the main floor of a church building. In some churches the crypt contains a chapel, a place of burial, or a columbarium; it suggests to some the early experience of the church when it had to hide in catacombs and the tombs of the martyrs served as altars.

Curate: A member of the clergy who has just been ordained and has his or her first position in a parish; this person is said to be serving a curacy in that place. May also mean the assisting clergy in a large parish, although usually after a new curate has been on the job for a while, he or she becomes the assistant rector or associate rector and leaves the title curate behind. The term was originally applied to the clergy in charge of a parish.

Cure of Souls: The word *cure* here comes from the same word which gives us the word *care*; therefore, the term refers to the people for whose spiritual health a member of the clergy is responsible. This may mean the members of a parish but may mean other groups if the clergyperson has a special ministry such as a chaplaincy or other nonparochial job.

Cursillo: Along with Faith Alive, Episcopal Marriage Encounter, and other movements, a spiritual renewal movement within the Episcopal Church. Cursillo is short for *Cursillos de Cristiandad,* Spanish words which can best be translated as "short courses in Christian living." The Cursillo movement began among Spanish Catholics in the 1940s, and spread to the United States and the Episcopal

Church in the 1950s and 1960s. Participants attend Cursillo weekends and then participate in continuing support groups when they return. The purpose of Cursillo is to train layfolk to bear witness to Christ in the daily environment.

D

Daily Office: Reading the Daily Office forms the basis of Anglican spirituality, as well as its life of prayer and reading of the Bible. Archbishop Cranmer set the pattern when he reduced the eight monastic services of prayer, reading, psalmody, and praise to two and put them in a book to be used by all clergy and layfolk. The Prayer Book of 1979 makes possible the observance of a four- or five-office day, adding An Order of Service for Noonday (BCP, 103-07); Evening, usually called vespers (BCP, 109-14); and Compline (BCP, 127-35) to Morning (BCP, 37-60, 75-102) and Evening Prayer (BCP, 61-73, 115-26), but the two basic Cranmerian offices remain the central ones. Also included are brief Daily Devotions for Individuals and Families for different times of day (BCP, 136-40), which follow the structure of the Daily Office. The Daily Office lectionary (BCP, 934-1001) is arranged in a two-year cycle of readings which takes the user through most of the Bible. The Psalms are repeated every seven weeks. The Offices also provide opportunity for Confession and Absolution and intercessory prayer. The Church Hymnal Society publishes a *Daily Office Book* and the *Daily Office Lessons* to facilitate observance of the Daily Offices. When the Offices are read publicly in churches, clergy wear cassocks, surplices, and tippets. With slight modifications described by the Prayer Book, the Offices can be led by deacons and layfolk as well as priests.

Dalmatic: A vestment worn by deacons when assisting at the altar, a tunic worn over an alb and stole; decorated with two colored strips of material that run vertically from front to back over the shoulders and are connected in the front and back by two horizontal strips of the same material. The dalmatic is a distinctive sign of the office of deacon, but may also be worn by priests when they are functioning as deacons at the altar (see **deacon**). Usually the dalmatic matches the chasuble worn by the celebrant in materials and colors. See also **tunicle.** [Figure 17]

Figure 17.   Deacon in Dalmatic

Deacon: Along with priests and bishops one of the three offices to which people can be ordained in the Episcopal Church. The diaconate is now being recovered as a full and equal order with special vocational concerns and emphases which only it can express. See BCP, 537-47, for the service of Ordination for a Deacon. The first deacons were ordained to help bishops with service to the poor and the distribution of alms; as a result, the diaconate's special emphasis is in serving, especially the weak, the poor, the sick, and the lonely, and in interpreting to the church the needs, concerns, and hopes of the world. The sign of the office of deacon is the stole, in the color of the season, worn over the left shoulder and fastened under the right arm. In the Eucharist, deacons read the Gospel, lead the Prayers of the People, issue the invitation to confession, prepare the altar, help with the distribution of the bread and wine, and proclaim the dismissal. In other services, deacons have special roles, such as chanting the Exsultet during the Easter Vigil. Deacons also preach and administer both the bread and the chalice at communion. They often take bread and wine from the reserved sacrament to those who cannot attend church services. Those who wish to become priests are also ordained deacons first, but those who seek diaconal orders alone to become vocational or permanent deacons are becoming an increasingly important part of the church's ministry. These vocational deacons go through a rigorous process, similar to that followed by those aspiring to the priesthood.

Dean: Title given to person holding any of three positions: (1) the head of a cathedral staff, (2) the head of a seminary faculty, (3) the clergyperson elected or appointed to preside over meetings of a geographical division of a diocese, called variously, in different parts of the church, a convocation, an archdeaconry, or a deanery. The title of a dean is The Very Reverend; the house a dean lives in is called a deanery.

Decalogue: The section of the Eucharist, Rite One, in which the Ten Commandments are repeated with responses; this is an optional part of Rite One (BCP, 317-18, 324), interchangeable with Christ's summary of the law. In Rite Two, it can be used as part of the Penitential Order preceding the Eucharist (BCP, 350-53).

Dedication of Churches: When an Episcopal parish first uses a building, the building is dedicated or consecrated for this purpose. See BCP, 567-79, for the text of the rite. After the dedication, the date on which it was held becomes the Feast of the Dedication for that parish, often a major celebration in parish life.

Deployment: The process by which ordained people are matched with specific congregations. There is a church deployment officer at national church headquarters in New York who works with a computer file of all clergy. This database lists each ordained person's background, preferences, experience, strengths, and other information. Once a parish has prepared a profile of the kind of person it seeks, it can use this database to get a list of clergy who fit its requirements. Many dioceses also have deployment officers who help clergy keep their deployment files (called CDO files) up to date, and assist parishes in clergy searches at a diocesan level.

Deputy: A person elected to represent a diocese at the General Convention of the Episcopal Church, which meets every three years. General Convention has two houses, the House of Bishops and the House of Deputies. The House of Deputies consists of four clerical and four lay deputies from each diocese, elected at a diocesan convention.

Devotions, Daily: For those who want a regular life of prayer for themselves or their families but who do not want to read the full Daily Office, the Prayer Book provides abbreviated services for morning, noon, early evening, and close of day (BCP, 136-40). Each consists of a set portion of the Psalter, a brief reading, prayers, and a collect.

Diocese: A geographical area which has a bishop, the diocese is the basic unit of administration in the Episcopal Church. Our church has 111 dioceses in North and South America comprising nine provinces, and an additional seven missionary dioceses in places like Liberia and the Philippines.

Diocesan Council: Body of lay and clerical members that serves between Diocesan Conventions to oversee the program of the diocese. Dioceses have some discretion in deciding how to choose the membership of the Council; in some dioceses, the members are elected by the Convention, while in others some members are elected by the Convention and others serve by virtue of their holding elected or appointed positions in the diocese. In any case, the Diocesan Council acts for the Diocesan Convention between its annual meetings.

Dismissal: Words spoken at the end of the Eucharist by a deacon or a priest if no deacon is present. These words instruct those present to "Go forth" (BCP, 339-40, 366). The dismissal in the medieval Latin rite was "Ite, missa est," meaning "Go forth; it is finished." In time, the word "missa" came to be the name of the thing that was finished, i.e., the Mass.

D. R. E., D. C. E.: Abbreviations, used almost universally, for director of religious education or director of Christian education, title for a person working in a parish or mission on a salaried or volunteer basis whose job is to organize and facilitate Christian education in that place.

Divine Liturgy: Another name for the Eucharist.

Dom: Title given to monks of the Benedictine Order. The most famous Anglican Benedictine of recent times was Dom Gregory Dix, whose *The Shape of the Liturgy* inspired and promoted the modern liturgical movement.

Dossal: A large piece of fabric, often decorated with symbols, which is hung on the wall behind the altar to serve as a kind of reredos. Where a dossal is part of the church furnishings, the parish may own several, and the dossal in use may match the liturgical color of the day.

Doxology: Any text that ascribes glory to the persons of the Trinity is a doxology, although the term is usually used for the phrase "Glory be to the Father and to the Son and to the Holy Spirit" used at the end of the Psalms and Canticles in

Morning and Evening Prayer. In many parishes the hymn verse which begins "Praise God from whom all blessings flow," sung at the time of the Offertory, is also referred to as the Doxology.

E

East: Traditionally, a church is built so that the altar is on the east side of the building, because Jesus promised that the Son of Man would come in glory on clouds from the east. On occasion, the altar end of the church is called the east end even if it is not geographically east. The baptismal font or the baptistry is traditionally in the westward end, to emphasize the claim that in baptism one moves out of darkness into light, but modern architecture usually places the font to the front and right of the sanctuary, across from the pulpit.

Easter: The day on which the church celebrates the feast of Christ's resurrection, Easter is the oldest and greatest feast in the church year and the central day on the liturgical calendar. Every Sunday is a "little Easter," since every Sunday is a Feast of the Resurrection. Easter Day is the culmination of Holy Week, with its special services recalling the last week of Jesus' earthly ministry; its observances are begun with the Easter Vigil and continue with the Eucharist on Easter Day. The liturgical color is white, or whatever is the color of the finest and most splendid vestment set owned by the parish. Easter Day begins the Easter season, which runs for fifty days until the Feast of Pentecost.

Easter Vigil: The central rite of the entire Christian year and a marvelously rich service (BCP, 285-95) which begins in darkness (any time convenient between Saturday sunset and Sunday sunrise) with the lighting of the new fire, from which the Paschal candle is lighted. A procession of clergy and servers follows this single light into the darkened church, pausing three times to chant, "The light of Christ." The Paschal candle is placed in its stand and, standing near it, a deacon or other person sings or says the Exsultet. The service continues with lessons which trace the history of God's people in the Old Testament; baptisms (or renewal of baptismal vows if there is no baptismal candidate); confirmation; and the first Eucharist of Easter. The Vigil service is especially impressive when it can include the initiatory rites, a deacon chanting the Exsultet, and a bishop celebrating the Eucharist with lay and clergy participating fully. Recovering the Easter Vigil in its full significance is one of the greatest achievements of the modern liturgical movement.

Elements: The bread and wine of the Eucharist.

Figure 18.   Priest Elevating
Bread and Wine

Elevation: Act of lifting the bread and wine at appropriate times during the Eucharist. In some places, the tradition is to elevate the bread and the wine in turn at the repetition of the words "he took" in the Eucharistic Prayer. In others, the bread and wine are elevated in turn after the words of institution, accompanied by a bow or a genuflection. Yet another place for an elevation, this time of both elements together, is at the conclusion of the canon at the words "Through Jesus Christ our Lord" or their equivalent. Finally, the bread may be elevated at the "Christ our Passover is sacrificed for us" (BCP, 337, 364), and both bread and wine may be elevated when the celebrant says, "The Gifts of God for the People of God" (BCP, 338, 364). [Figure 18]

Ember Days: Four groups of three days, specifically the Wednesday, Friday, and Saturday after the First Sunday in Lent, Pentecost, Holy Cross Day (September 14), and St. Lucy's Day (December 13), which were set aside long ago as special days for fasting. They seem to have been created to take over pagan festivals connected with the annual cycle of the seasons and harvests. They are of such age that although we no longer have St. Lucy's Day on our calendar, we still have the Ember Days associated with her feast day. Now, the Ember Days are hardly noticed except by seminarians and their bishops, because seminarians are required to write their bishops Ember Day letters at each of the Ember seasons. These seasons are popular occasions for ordinations.

Enquirers' Class: Study group in preparation for Confirmation, Reception, or the Renewal of Baptismal Vows; also known as a confirmation class.

Entrance Rite: The first part of the Eucharist, in which the people gather in the name of God. It includes the opening Acclamation, the Collect for Purity, the Gloria or other hymn, and the Collect for the Day (BCP, 323-25, 355-57).

Epiklesis, Epiclesis: From Greek word meaning "to call down"; used to designate the moment in the Great Thanksgiving or Eucharistic Prayer when the celebrant asks that the Holy Spirit sanctify the bread and wine that they may be "for your people the Body and Blood of your Son." Frequently associated with a manual act by the celebrant in which the hands are held together over the elements or the sign of the cross is made over them.

Epiphany: The Feast of the Epiphany is January 6, and the Epiphany season runs from January 6 until Ash Wednesday, the beginning of Lent. The liturgical color is white, until after the First Sunday after the Epiphany, when it becomes green. *Epiphany* means "revealing" or "showing forth," and the Epiphany season begins with the showing forth of Jesus (the extension of his ministry) to the Gentiles, specifically to the wise men of Matthew's Gospel, who are the first to know of his divinity. Epiphany thus proclaims Jesus as Savior of the whole world and prepares for the proclamation that the church is the new people of God, with God's promises of salvation now applying to all the peoples of the earth.

Episcopal: Pertaining to a bishop. Thus we are the Episcopal Church because we have bishops. The ring worn by a bishop as the sign of his office is his episcopal ring.

Episcopal Church, The: One of the official names of the institution this book is about; the other is The Protestant Episcopal Church in the United States of America.

Episcopal Church Annual: An annual publication of the church which functions as a directory to the church in all its constituent parts, listing names and addresses of all national officers and agencies, along with the bishops and their diocesan headquarters, the various conference and retreat centers, monastic orders, health and welfare agencies, and the clergy of the church. Also included is a list of the names and office addresses of the constituent churches of the Anglican communion.

Episcopal Church Flag, Seal: The familiar Episcopal Church flag and seal, adopted by the General Convention in 1940, display the same symbols. The red cross that divides the white field into four rectangles is the cross of St. George, the patron saint of England. The colors red, white, and blue are the colors of the flags of both the United States and England. The blue field to the upper left contains a cross made of nine crosslets. The composite cross is the cross of St. Andrew, the patron saint of Scotland. Each of the nine crosslets which make up the cross of St. Andrew represents one of the nine dioceses which met in Philadelphia in 1789 to form the Protestant Episcopal Church in the United States of America. The cross of St. Andrew remembers the fact that Samuel Seabury, first bishop of the Episcopal Church, was consecrated by bishops of the Anglican Church of Scotland. The nine founding dioceses were the dioceses of Connecticut, New York, Maryland, Massachusetts, Pennsylvania, New Jersey, Delaware, Virginia, and South Carolina. The flag and seal thus reveal the heritage of the Episcopal Church with its origins in both England and Scotland. [Figures 18a, 18b]

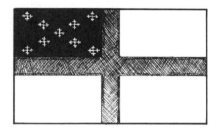

Figure 18a.   Episcopal Flag

Figure 18b.
Episcopal Seal

Episcopal Church Women, or ECW: A national organization for women Episcopalians which has chapters in most parishes. The national organization holds a convention every three years called the Triennial, which is held in the same year as the General Convention of the church. Diocesan ECWs hold conventions annually.

Episcopal Clergy Association: National professional organization of Episcopal clergy; holds annual conventions and publishes a newsletter called *Leaven.* Many dioceses also have local chapters of the ECA.

Episcopal Clerical Directory: Book published every two years which gives the names, addresses, and brief biographical sketches of all the ordained people in the Episcopal Church.

Episcopal Young Churchpeople or EYC: Organization for junior high and high school youth in a parish. Frequently a parish will have a Junior EYC and an EYC (for high school students).

Episcopalian: A member of the Episcopal Church. *Episcopalian* is a noun. *Episcopal* is an adjective.

Episcopate: The function or rank of bishops, collectively. Thus the office held by bishops is the episcopate, while the office held by priests is the priesthood, and the office held by deacons is the diaconate. Also used in the phrase, "the historic episcopate," referring to the tradition of vesting in bishops the office of providing continuity from age to age in the church.

Epistle: The second of three readings at the Eucharist, because it is usually from the New Testament Epistles. The first lesson is usually from the Old Testament, and the third lesson is always from one of the Gospels.

Epistoler: Lay reader who reads the Epistle; may vest in an alb (and tunicle) and function as the subdeacon.

Eucharist: From the Greek word meaning "thanksgiving"; now perhaps the most common name for what is also known as the Holy Communion, the Lord's Supper, or the Mass.

72

The Eucharist is the identifying act of the Christian community, what the Prayer Book calls "the principal act of Christian worship on the Lord's Day, and other major Feasts" (BCP, 13). It is found in the Prayer Book in two full versions, one in traditional language called Rite One (BCP, 323-49) and one in contemporary language called Rite Two (BCP, 355-82), as well as a "Rite Three" Order for Eucharist (BCP, 400-05) for use on special occasions and under special circumstances such as a retreat when it is desirable to have a celebration closely linked to the occasion and less formal than either Rite One or Two. The Eucharist is the sacrament of Christ's resurrection and his ongoing presence at work among us; it also anticipates the eschatological banquet through which Christ's lordship is proclaimed to all and his promises fulfilled. The Eucharist has two major divisions—the Liturgy of the Word (for Bible reading, preaching, prayer of intercession, confession, and the Passing of the Peace) and the Liturgy of the Eucharist (in which the bread and wine are offered and blessed, the bread is broken, and all receive).

Eucharistic Prayer: The Great Thanksgiving, the prayer over the bread and wine in the Eucharist, beginning with the salutation and preface, and continuing to the doxology and amen; see also **canon, Eucharist, Great Thanksgiving.**

Eucharistic Vestments: Distinctive garments worn during the Eucharist. For the celebrant, eucharistic vestments consist of an alb, girdle, stole, and chasuble, although the celebrant may wear a cope for the entrance procession and until the Offertory. A full set of eucharistic vestments for a deacon would consist of an alb, amice, girdle, stole, and dalmatic, although in parishes with limited vestment funds, the dalmatic is often not seen. A lay chalice bearer serving as subdeacon may wear alb, amice, girdle, and tunicle, or, like the deacon, may leave off the outer garment. In some parishes, the tradition is for the celebrant to wear a cassock, surplice, and stole instead of the other eucharistic vestments.

Evaluation: Many parishes conduct an annual evaluation of the work of the clergy and the vestry to help ensure that the basic purposes of ministry in the congregation are being pursued effectively with a sense of mutual accountability.

Evening Prayer, Evensong: The second of two Daily Offices created by Archbishop Cranmer in the original Prayer Book of 1549 and continued in all Prayer Books since (BCP, 61-73, 115-26). Evening Prayer consists of Opening Sentences, an optional Confession and Absolution, reading from the Psalter, one or more Lessons with Canticles, the Apostles' Creed, Suffrages, and Prayers. The service may be combined with the Order of Worship for the Evening (BCP, 109-14); it may also be sung, in part, to become a real "even-song."

Ewer: Container of water for use at Baptism or on Maundy Thursday at the Washing of Feet. See also **flagon.**

Executive Council: The body which oversees the business of the national Episcopal Church between General Conventions, the Executive Council meets three or four times a year on a regular basis, and more often if necessary. It has forty-five members and consists of the Presiding Bishop (president and chair), the president of the House of Deputies (vice-chair), a treasurer, the secretary of the General Convention, and a group of lay and ordained members who are elected at large and by province. The members are divided into a number of standing committees which have oversight responsibility for such areas of the church's life as stewardship, national and world mission, and education. To help them in their work, the council employs a staff which operates the national headquarters of the Episcopal Church at 815 Second Avenue, New York, N.Y. 10017.

Exhortation: When Thomas Cranmer created the first Prayer Book, he faced a situation in which people were so accustomed to watching the Eucharist celebrated and not receiving that the ordinary layperson rarely received more than once or twice a year. As a result, he provided in the Prayer Book appeals to receive the Eucharist more frequently. A combining of his appeals into a single text is found on pages 316-17 of the Prayer Book, and similar statements which seek to set the proper tone for what follows can be found as part of the rite for Ash Wednesday (BCP, 264-65) as well as before Confession at Morning Prayer (BCP, 41, 79).

Exsultet: Song of rejoicing and giving thanks for "this night" and remembering central moments in the history of God's people, sung or said by a deacon or other person appointed after the lighting of the Paschal candle and procession into the church during the Easter Vigil (BCP, 286-87).

F

Fabric of the Church: The buildings and furniture of a parish. Some parishes have standing committees of people expert in the preservation and repair of these, especially when the church building is of historic significance.

Fair Linen: White linen cloth about the width of the altar but long enough to cover the top of the altar with some overhang at the ends; another name for the altar cloth. At the Offertory, the corporal is placed upon the fair linen and then the chalice and paten are placed on the corporal for a celebration of the Eucharist. The name is traditional; Cranmer's first Prayer Book called for a "fair linen" cloth to be placed on the altar, and the name has endured.

Fasts, Fasting: The Prayer Book defines certain days as fast days, or "days observed by special acts of discipline and self-denial": (1) Ash Wednesday and the other weekdays of Lent and of Holy Week, except for the Feast of the Annunciation (March 25), and (2) Good Friday and all other Fridays of the year, except for Fridays in the Christmas and Easter seasons, and any feasts of our Lord which happen to occur on a Friday. The reason for fast days is to help us discern what really matters to us, to prepare for the great celebration of Easter and all the "little Easters"—the Sundays of the year.

Feasts: Certain days defined by the Prayer Book, including (1) all Sundays; (2) the movable feasts, especially Easter and Pentecost and others which vary from year to year as the date of Easter moves; and (3) the immovable feasts, including Christmas, Epiphany, All Saints' Day, and the days for commemorating the saints. Sundays take precedence over saints' days and force them to be transferred to other days (BCP, 16-17).

Fire, New: The lighting of the "new fire" in the darkness of Easter Eve is a part of the Easter Vigil (BCP, 285), where the fire is blessed and used to light the Paschal candle. The Easter Vigil is a rite of new beginnings. It celebrates the beginning of our new life in the risen Christ, the light springing up in darkness, so the new fire is an appropriate way to begin this rite of new beginnings.

First Communion: In the past, one had to be confirmed to receive the Eucharist. With the renewed emphasis on Baptism as the full and complete sacrament of initiation into the Christian community, however, this requirement no longer holds. In some places everyone receives from Baptism on, so that children will never remember when they were not welcome at the Lord's table. In other places it is felt that children should wait until they have some idea of the Eucharist's meaning. In these places, at the desired age children receive instruction and their First Communion is made a special occasion. Even within parishes, practice differs among families.

Flagon: Large metal or ceramic pitcher used for wine or water at the Eucharist.

Fifty Days of Easter: The Easter season; runs for fifty days, from Easter Sunday until the Day of Pentecost.

Font: A special container for the water of Baptism. In traditionally arranged churches the font is near the west end of the building, near the entrance, to remind us that Baptism is the rite of full entry into the church. The term *font* is also used for a fixed holy water receptacle found at the entrance of some churches. [Figure 19]

Figure 19.   Baptismal Font

Fraction: The moment in the Eucharist when the celebrant breaks the bread (BCP, 337, 364).

Friar: A member of a religious order which identifies itself with the medieval orders founded by St. Francis of Assisi. In the Episcopal Church, this would include the Society of St. Francis, with headquarters in Mt. Sinai, N.Y., and the Brotherhood of St. Gregory, with headquarters in the Bronx, N.Y.

Frontal: A panel of embroidered cloth which covers the altar on the front or on all sides. It usually has as its dominant color one of the seasonal colors and is replaced by another frontal of an appropriate color when the liturgical color of the day or season changes. The altar cloth, or fair linen, is spread over the top and sides of the frontal. [Plates A and B]

General Convention: The official governing body of the Episcopal Church. General Convention meets every three years for a period of ten days to two weeks; recently it has met in 1979, 1982, and 1985. Delegates to the convention sit in two legislative bodies, the House of Bishops (chaired by the Presiding Bishop) and the House of Deputies (chaired by its president). All bishops of the church, whether they are retired, diocesan, coadjutors, or suffragans, sit in the House of Bishops. Delegates to the House of Deputies (four clergy and four lay from each diocese) are elected at Diocesan Conventions. The General Convention requires the approval of both houses for any action to be passed; measures may originate in either house, except that the House of Bishops elects the Presiding Bishop with the concurrence of the House of Deputies. The agenda of General Convention varies from matters of program and policy to decisions about the Prayer Book and church policy on questions of theology and ethics. While most issues can be dealt with at a single convention, basic questions such as the form of the Prayer Book or the *Hymnal* or changes in the Constitution of the Church take the vote of two consecutive conventions. Between conventions, the business of the church is carried out by the Executive Council.

General Thanksgiving: Prayer first appearing in Thomas Cranmer's Prayer Book of 1549 which is part of Morning and Evening Prayer (BCP, 58-59, 71-72, 101, 125); so called because in it we give thanks generally for "all [God's] goodness and loving-kindness."

Figure 20. Genuflection

Genuflection: An act of reverence that involves kneeling so that the right knee touches the floor and then standing up again. In parishes where this is part of the tradition, parishioners genuflect when passing by a tabernacle or aumbry in which the reserved sacrament is being kept (signaled by a sanctuary lamp burning white rather than red); when entering or leaving the seating area when consecrated bread or wine is on the altar (such as when going to receive); and when the words "for us and for our salvation" are said in the Nicene Creed. Clergy may also observe these moments and add genuflections during the prayer of consecration after the words of institution over each element and after the great "Amen" at the end of the prayer. Since bowing at these moments is an older tradition than genuflecting and in fact was almost universal in England at the time of the Reformation, many now observe that tradition. [Figure 20]

Girdle: A rope, frequently with tassels on the ends, worn around the waist over an alb. Basically the girdle is brought around the waist and tied with a slip knot so that the ends hang down the wearer's left side. When the celebrant vests, however, he or she loops the girdle back over itself on either

80

side of the knot to provide places through which to pass the celebrant's stole, which is either crossed at the waist or hangs straight on each side from the neck; in either case the stole is usually held by the girdle to prevent it from getting in the celebrant's way.

Gloria in Excelsis: Opening Latin words and therefore popular name for the great eucharistic hymn "Glory to God in the Highest" (BCP, 324, 356). The hymn is used from Christmas Day through the Feast of the Epiphany, on the Sundays from Easter Day through the Feast of Pentecost, every day of Easter Week, on Ascension Day, and any other time it seems appropriate. However, it is never used on Sundays or ordinary weekdays in the penitential seasons of Advent and Lent (BCP, 406).

Gloria Patri: Opening Latin words and therefore popular name for the ascription of praise to the Trinity that runs "Glory to the Father and to the Son and to the Holy Spirit: as it was in the beginning, is now, and will be forever. Amen." Used after the reciting of Psalms and after the Canticles in the Daily Offices.

Good Friday: Friday before Easter, on which we remember the crucifixion of Jesus with a day of fasting, abstinence, penance, and special devotion. Special rites for the day (BCP, 276-82) include a reading of the passion narrative from John's Gospel, a lengthy period of intercessory prayer called the Solemn Collects, and the recitation of anthems recalling the significance of the cross. No Eucharist is celebrated this day; the altars were stripped at the end of the Eucharist on Maundy Thursday and any immovable crosses were shrouded. In some places a cross is brought forward during the Good Friday liturgy to serve as a focus for devotion. Communion may be part of the Good Friday liturgy, but it is administered from the reserved sacrament. No celebration of the Eucharist, in fact, takes place from

Maundy Thursday until the celebration at the Easter Vigil on Easter Eve.

Godparents: Witnesses to a Christian Baptism who make the baptismal promises in the name of the child and who assume responsibility for insuring that the child is brought up in the faith of the church (see BCP, 301-06 for an outline of the liturgical role of godparents). For older children and adults, they are called sponsors (BCP, 298).

Gospel: The third reading from the Bible at the Eucharist, which is always taken from one of the four Gospels. The Gospel is appropriately read by a deacon if one is present, or by a priest, and is followed immediately by the sermon. In some places reading of the Gospel is specially marked by having acolytes holding candles stand near the lectern, or the Gospel book can be brought into the middle of the congregation by a Gospel procession. All stand for the reading of the Gospel, turning toward the reader.

Gospel Book: A book which contains only the Gospel lessons appointed for the Eucharist. This may be handsomely decorated and is designed to be a processional, ceremonial book.

Gospel Procession: The carrying of the Gospel book into the middle of the congregation so that the Gospel may be proclaimed in the midst of the people. This may be done by the reader of the Gospel, or it may be a real procession involving acolytes with candles and the use of incense. In such a procession, the Gospel book or Bible could be carried by the subdeacon who would hold it for the reader.

Gospeler: The deacon or priest who reads the Gospel.

Gradine: A ledge or shelf above and behind a traditional altar located against the wall of the church building on which the cross and candlesticks are sometimes placed. [Plate A]

Gradual: Hymn, Psalm, or anthem sung by congregation or choir between the Epistle and the Gospel in the Eucharist. Generally the portion of the Psalter appointed for a day is used between the Old Testament Lesson and the Epistle and the place of the gradual is taken by a congregational hymn or an anthem sung by a choir.

Great Litany: A litany is a long intercessory rite involving extensive use of versicles and responses. The Great Litany (BCP, 148-55) is not only an important liturgical text for us, but was the very first English-language rite created by Archbishop Cranmer as he set about in the 1540s to make worship in English possible. It was originally written to be sung in procession but is now appropriately said or sung in procession, or standing, or kneeling, at any time during the church year, before the Eucharist or after the Collects of Morning or Evening Prayer, or as a rite by itself. It is frequently done in Lent, on Rogation Days, or on the First Sunday of Advent. When we pray the Great Litany, we are in a way participating again in the creation of our heritage as Anglican Christians.

Great Thanksgiving: Official name for the Prayer of Consecration, which begins with the salutation or Sursum Corda and ends with the Lord's Prayer.

H

Habit: The distinctive clothing worn by members of religious orders; a distinctive outward sign of the religious life. Traditionally it consists of a tunic, belt or girdle, scapular (a sleeveless cloak hanging almost to the feet), hood for men (monks and friars) and veil for women (nuns), and a mantle. Recently, at least in the case of some religious orders, variations generally in the form of simplification have joined the traditional forms of dress. Some orders have dispensed with the traditional clothing altogether or created an updated version. A nun, for example, may wear a plain contemporary dress with a simplified version of the traditional veil instead of the full traditional habit.

Hail Mary: First words of the prayer to the Blessed Virgin Mary used especially in the saying of the Rosary. The Hail Mary combines two biblical texts, the words of the angel to Mary at the Annunciation and the words of her cousin Elizabeth to Mary at the Visitation, both from Luke (1: 28 and 42), and a petition that Mary pray for us. The usual translation runs as follows: "Hail, Mary, full of grace. The Lord is with thee. Blessed art thou among women, and blessed is the fruit of thy womb, Jesus. Holy Mary, Mother of God, pray for us sinners, now and at the hour of our death."

Hands, Laying on of: Action especially associated with conveying the Holy Spirit; used by priests in Baptism (BCP, 308) and Ministration to the Sick (BCP, 455-57) and by bishops in the Confirmation and Ordination rites (BCP, 418, 521, 533, 545). Priests join the bishop in the Laying on of Hands at Ordination to the priesthood.

Hangings: All the various fabric adornments for the lectern, pulpit, altar, etc., which are made in the liturgical colors and changed as the colors change.

Healing, Service of: A public version of the rite of Ministration to the Sick which provides for prayer, readings from the Bible, and the Laying on of Hands and Anointing (BOS, 147-54); although it is designed to be part of a Eucharist, it may be performed alone.

Hierarchy: The structure of governance in the Episcopal Church in which authority is distributed according to ascending rank. In the clergy, priests and deacons acknowledge the authority of the bishop of the diocese. The laity also acknowledge the authority of the bishop, but give authority in parish life to the vestry, and in diocesan life to the Diocesan Convention and to the Standing Committee and the Diocesan Council.

High Altar: In a church building with several altars, the altar which is centrally and most prominently located is the high altar. It traditionally stands at the east end of the building. [Plate C]

High Mass: In parishes where the Eucharist is referred to as the Mass, a celebration in which the celebrant is joined by someone functioning as deacon and someone as subdeacon is called a High Mass. When only the celebrant stands at the altar, it is a Low Mass. The High Mass model for a celebration is the most ancient, the Low Mass model developing only when priests adopted the weekly or daily discipline of celebrating the mass. The High Mass is usually accompanied by an especially rich ceremonial and elaborate music, but does not have to be. This style of celebrating the Eucharist is now becoming known as a Solemn Eucharist as well as High Mass.

Holy Communion: Traditional Episcopal name for the Eucharist, now used specifically for its second part, beginning with the Offertory (BCP, 333, 361), following the Liturgy of the Word. May still be used to refer to the whole service.

Holy Days: Days on the calendar of the church other than Sundays which are designated for special observance, including celebrations of events in the life of Jesus, days for remembering the apostles, evangelists, and other saints, and days of national significance like Independence Day and Thanksgiving. For a full list, see BCP, 16-18.

Holy Oil: As distinct from chrism, which is blessed by the bishop for use in Baptism, holy oil is blessed by a priest for use in public and private rites of healing (BCP, 455; BOS, 151).

Holy Orders: The three orders of ordained ministry in the Episcopal Church—bishops, priests, and deacons.

Holy Saturday: The day before Easter, commemorating the resting of Christ's body in the tomb. There is no celebration of the Eucharist on this day; BCP, 283 provides lessons and a Collect for a Liturgy of the Word.

Holy Water: Water that has been blessed; relates to the water of Baptism. It is found in some churches in a holy water stoup or bowl on the wall at the entrance to the building; those entering dip the fingers of their right hand into it and make the sign of the cross in an act of self-cleansing. Holy water may also be sprinkled on the congregation by the celebrant, using an aspergillum, during the procession to the altar before the Eucharist, or on the casket at a burial, or through a house being blessed. In each case, the action suggests a cleansing and a setting apart for a liturgically related purpose.

Holy Week: The last week of Lent and the week before Easter, in which the events in the last week of Jesus' earthly ministry are remembered. The Prayer Book provides special services for most of these days and special readings for all of them. The week begins with Passion Sunday, traditionally called Palm Sunday, with its blessing of palms and procession, followed by a reading of the passion narrative from one of the synoptic Gospels. The Book of Occasional Services (73-90) contains the service of Tenebrae for use on the Wednesday evening before Easter as a focused meditation in preparation for the remembrance of Christ's passion. This powerful service takes its name from the Latin word for "darkness" and provides for a series of readings and responses; gradually the lights and candles used to decorate the church are extinguished so that all is in darkness. A loud noise is made, recalling the earthquake at the time of the crucifixion. A single candle is lighted to aid the departure of the congregation. On Thursday, called Maundy Thursday, the church remembers Christ's institution of the Eucharist (BCP, 274-75) and, in some places, observes the ceremony of the washing of feet in remembrance of Jesus' washing the feet of his disciples. The name *Maundy* may be a shortened form of the word *commandment* in its early spelling *commaundement*; the Gospel associated with this day is of Jesus' saying to his disciples, "I give you a new commandment: Love one another as I have loved you." *Maundy* may also be a shortened form of the Latin words for "new commandment"—*mandatum novum*. Some places observe the time between noon and three on Good Friday with a three-hour preaching service; the Prayer Book provides a rite with extensive intercessory prayer and Anthems (BCP, 276-82) and provision for the traditional veneration of the cross. When this is done with a full-sized cross which members of the congregation take turns holding, it can be very powerful indeed. There is no celebration of the Eucharist on Good Friday or Holy Saturday, but lessons and prayers are provided for a Liturgy of the Word (BCP, 283) during the day on Holy Saturday. The whole week's liturgical activities lead to the Great Vigil of Easter (BCP, 285-95), with its lighting of the new fire and Paschal candle, reading of the salvation history, chanting of the Exsultet, Baptisms, Confirmations if the bishop is present, and the first Eucharist of Easter. This is, of course, followed by the Eucharists of Easter Day itself. The week can also be enhanced by use of the Way of the Cross service—also known as the Stations of the Cross (BOS, 55-71)—which may also be used on the Fridays of Lent. Holy Week is the central week of the whole liturgical year.

Homily: A sermon; sometimes used to suggest an address at sermon-time felt to be shorter and more informal than a fully developed sermon, but that usage seeks to create a difference when none exists.

Host: The wafers of unleavened bread used in some parishes at the Eucharist; the large one elevated by the priest and broken at the Fraction is called the priest's host, and the smaller ones distributed to the congregation are called people's hosts.

Hours: The services that mark the passage of time in the devotional day. In the Middle Ages, the eight hours had names taken from the times of their performance, like *none* for noonday. The Prayer Book provides for a four-office devotional day with Morning Prayer, Noonday Prayer, Evening Prayer, and Compline. In the early days of the Anglican Church, Morning and Evening Prayer were said at the "canonical hours" of ten and four.

House Blessing: Traditional name for the service of Celebration for a Home (BOS, 131-41), which involves prayers, readings, a Blessing of the Home, a Eucharist, and, best of all, a procession through the house with a stop in each room for a collect. This may be accompanied with liberal distribution of incense and holy water and be followed by a grand party. A house blessing is a splendid occasion to invite the entire parish to your house, introduce them to your neighbors and colleagues from work, and build community.

Humble Access, Prayer of: Traditional name for the prayer in the Eucharist, Rite One (BCP, 337) that begins "We do not presume to come to this thy Table, O merciful Lord."

Hymn: A religious poem set to music so that it may be sung by a congregation during worship. Hymn singing has been an important part of worship in the Episcopal Church only since the nineteenth century, but the Episcopal *Hymnal* is now one of the standard collections. The General Convention of 1982 approved a new hymnal, providing music for the rites of the Prayer Book of 1979 and supplementing the *Hymnal* of 1940.

I

Incense: Pellets of aromatic gum which are burned in a thurible or censer, a metal pot, usually of brass, into which disks of charcoal are placed and lighted. When the charcoal is hot, the gum is spooned into the thurible from its container (an incense boat) and the perforated cover of the thurible is lowered. As the incense pellets burn, they emit a pungent aroma and smoke. Incense has been part of Christian worship since the beginning; today, in parishes where its use is part of local ceremonial, it is carried in procession, and is also employed to prepare both priest and people for worship, at the reading of the Gospel and the preparation of the altar for celebration of the Eucharist, to contribute to the honor, festivity, and solemnity of the occasion. See illustration at **thurible.** [Figure 36]

Institution, Letter of: Letter from the bishop of a diocese authorizing a priest to exercise ministry in a parish to which he or she has been called (BCP, 557).

Institution, Words of: See **words of institution.**

Intercessions: Prayers of petition for the needs of the world. Often used to mean specifically the Prayers of the People, one of the essential parts of the Eucharist, the offering of the concerns of the congregation to God. Set forms for this are found in BCP, 328-29 and 383-95.

Intinction: Method of receiving the Eucharist in which the parishioner or the person administering the wine takes the bread (usually a wafer) and dips it into the chalice so that the parishioner can eat the moistened bread. Some people do this if they are worried about getting germs from drinking from a common cup; others do it if they have colds to try to avoid spreading their germs through the chalice.

Introit: Musical part of the entrance rite at the Eucharist, traditionally consisting of a portion of the Psalter, an Antiphon, and the Gloria Patri, but a sung Psalm or hymn at the entrance of the clergy can also be considered an introit.

Investiture: Short name for the service (BOS, 217-23) in which a previously consecrated bishop assumes a new role as bishop of a diocese.

Invitatory: Canticle said or sung at Morning and Evening Prayer after the opening versicle and response and before the selection from the Psalter (BCP, 44-46 and 82-84, 64 and 118).

J

Jesse Tree: A symbol often found in windows and other places of decoration in the church. Jesus was of the house and lineage of David; therefore he was a descendant of Jesse, David's father, and a part of his family tree. Lately, the Jesse tree symbol has taken on a new role as an aid to devotion in Advent. Functioning like the Advent calendar, the Jesse tree provides for each day in Advent a story from the Old Testament of one of Jesus' forebears and a symbol that can be cut out and attached to a tree of some sort. This can be a highly effective center for family devotions in Advent in conjunction with the Advent wreath.

Jubilate, or Jubilate Deo: Latin for "O be joyful," the beginning of Psalm 100; used as a Canticle in Morning Prayer (BCP, 45, 82-83).

K

Kerygma: Greek word for "preaching." It is used in the Church to refer to the Church's proclamation about Jesus: that he is the Christ, the Lord, the Son of God, in and through whom God acts decisively for the redemption of the world. This word is used to distinguish such proclamation from instruction in the Christian life, which is referred to by another Greek word, *didache*.

Kiss of Peace, Exchange of Peace: An ancient greeting between Christians, the kiss of peace became part of the eucharistic liturgy by the second century and has been recovered in the Prayer Book in the exchange of greeting called The Peace (BCP, 332, 360); usually now accompanied by a handshake, or a ritualized clasping of hands, embrace, or kiss.

Kneeling: Posture appropriate for, but not necessary to, penitential moments in the rites of the church such as Confession. Traditionally Episcopalians knelt to pray and receive the Eucharist, stood to sing, and sat to listen. Since the Eucharist is a sign of our freedom in Christ, many now find it more appropriate to stand to pray intercessory prayers and to receive the Eucharist. In Rite Two, the Prayer Book directs the congregation to stand for the opening rite, to sit for the first two Lessons, and stand for the Gospel and the Creed. No specific directions are provided for the Intercessions and the Confession, except that the celebrant must stand to pronounce absolution. The option of standing or kneeling is provided for the Eucharistic Prayer, but no further specific directions are provided. Rite One retains the direction that all kneel for the Confession in one version of the invitation to Confession (BCP, 330) but not the other. Perhaps the best thing to say here is that body posture in the church is now evolving within the limits provided by Prayer Book directives, that different parishes will behave differently in this regard, and that within any congregation worshipers feel free to assume the posture indicative of each person's sense of what is appropriate. [Figure 21]

Figure 21.   Kneeling

Kyrie Eleison: Greek for "Lord, have mercy," a traditional text read or sung as part of the entrance rite at the Eucharist, sometimes together with the Gloria in Excelsis (Rite One: BCP, 324) or instead of it in penitential seasons (Rite Two: BCP, 356).

L

Lady Chapel: A side chapel dedicated to Saint Mary the Virgin in a large church.

Laity: From the Greek *laos,* meaning "people." The laity is really all the people of God, including the nonordained and the ordained, but conventionally the word is used to refer to nonordained Christians. Only members of the laity can be elected to vestries or vote in the lay order at Diocesan Convention or General Convention.

Laity, Ministry of the: All of the people of God are called to further God's reconciling work in the world. Unfortunately, many hold the clergy to be the ministers or professional Christians for the congregation. Recently the renewal of emphasis on Baptism as full initiation into the Christian life has revived a sense of the importance of ministry for all the congregation. Christian ministry takes place in the world wherever Christians live, work, and play with their families, friends, and colleagues. It is not just lay reading or working on parish committees, although those things are important. A number of programs have been developed to help layfolk discover and claim their ministries.

Lambeth Conference: Meeting of the bishops of all twenty-one autonomous churches in the Anglican communion, called every ten years by the Archbishop of Canterbury, who chairs the sessions. The name comes from the fact that the meetings are held at Lambeth Palace in London. The

Lambeth Conference is one major way in which the relationships among member churches of the Anglican communion are developed and maintained. At its meetings, matters of mutual concern are studied and resolutions of an advisory nature are passed. The Lambeth Conference has only advisory power, but its opinions do have great influence on the decisions of member churches of the Anglican communion.

Lambeth Palace: The London residence and office of the Archbishop of Canterbury. Located on the south bank of the Thames River, its address is Lambeth Palace, London SE1 9JU England.

Lambeth Quadrilateral: Statement approved by Anglican bishops at the Lambeth Conference of 1888 concerning what the Anglican communion held were the essential marks of the one holy catholic and apostolic church and thus the essential requirements of any reunited Christian church. These are (1) the Holy Scriptures of the Old and New Testaments as containing all things necessary for salvation and as being the rule and standard of the faith, (2) the Apostles' Creed as the baptismal symbol and the Nicene Creed as the sufficient statement of the Christian faith, (3) the two sacraments of Baptism and Eucharist, and (4) the historic episcopate as the symbol of the unity of the church. See BCP, 876-78, for the actual text of the Lambeth Quadrilateral and of the Chicago Quadrilateral of 1886, a fuller statement on the same subject passed by the General Convention of 1886.

Lamp: Large candle holders, usually hanging from the ceiling or fixed on stands, found around the altar in the sanctuary of a church, thus often called sanctuary lamps. Where the consecrated bread and wine of the Eucharist are kept in an aumbry or tabernacle in reservation, a lamp is usually placed before the location and burns white when the sacrament is present, or red when it is not.

Lavabo: Latin word meaning "I will wash"; in this context refers to a ceremonial washing of the celebrant's fingers before the Eucharistic Prayer, usually facilitated by a server who holds a basin (the lavabo bowl), a cruet of water, and a towel (the lavabo towel) and pours water over the celebrant's fingers as they are held over the bowl. This ceremony is customary in some parishes and not in others.

Lay Chalice Bearer: See **chalice bearer.**

Lay Ministry: The Catechism calls ministry the means through which the church carries out its mission, which is "to restore all people to unity with God and each other in Christ." It also defines those with a ministry in the church as "all its members," ordained and lay. In brief, the ministry of layfolk is to represent and bear witness to Christ and his church, to carry on Christ's reconciling work in the world, and to take their place in the life, worship and governance of the church. Many people think of the parish as the arena for ministry and of lay ministry as working in positions of responsibility in the parish. While this is certainly true, the arena for the conduct of ministry also includes the work, community, and family settings in which people live out their vocations. The Catechism concludes by defining the duty of all Christians as "to follow Christ; to come together week by week for corporate worship; and to work, pray, and give for the spread of the kingdom of God."

Lay Order: Body of delegates to a diocesan convention or General Convention composed of the laypersons elected to represent their parishes or dioceses. The distinction between the lay order and the clerical order becomes important in votes on controversial issues. Votes are usually taken by voice, with clergy and laity voting at once, but anyone can call for a vote by orders. In that case, the votes are cast in each order, and the measure has to pass in both orders before it is considered to be approved.

Lay Reader: Layperson licensed by the bishop to read in church. The lay reader usually goes through a period of study before licensing and reads the Old Testament, Epistle, and Intercessions during the Eucharist. In the absence of a priest, such as during the time a parish is searching for a new rector, the lay readers may read Morning and Evening Prayer and preach approved lay readers' sermons.

Figure 22.   Bishop Laying On Hands

Laying on of Hands: Action especially associated with the conveyance of the Holy Spirit, used by priests in Baptism (BCP, 308) and Ministration to the Sick (BCP, 455-56) and by bishops in the Confirmation and Ordination rites (BCP, 418, 521, 533, 545). [Figure 22]

Lectern: Stand for holding a book during the reading of lessons; may also be used as a place for preaching. Lecterns in Episcopal churches may be very simple stands, or they may be elaborate structures with eagles holding the book stand in their wings. [Plate C]

Lector: One who reads lessons from the lectionary at a lectern. This is a name of a role, so that the lector could be a lay person or an ordained person.

Lectionary: A list of lessons from the Bible to be read at certain specific times. The BCP actually contains two lectionaries, (1) the eucharistic lectionary (BCP, 889-931), which provides for reading large sections of the Bible over a three-year cycle of readings at the Eucharist, and (2) the Daily Office lectionary (BCP, 934-1001), which provides for reading practically all of the Bible over a two-year cycle of readings at Morning and Evening Prayer. See also **calendar.**

Lent: The season of the church year that runs for forty weekdays and six Sundays between Ash Wednesday and Easter and is a special season of preparation for Easter. The liturgical colors are purple or the natural color of unbleached linen. The penitential tone of the season is reflected in the prohibition of the singing of the Gloria in Excelsis during Lent. Many people observe Lent by undertaking special programs of study; many practice self-denial. The purpose of Lent is not self-punishment but preparation for Easter through concentration on fundamental values and priorities.

Lenten Array: Some parishes follow an old tradition and use unbleached linen or sackcloth for vestments, coverings, and hangings during Lent. These may have red trim and bear symbols of Christ's Passion in red and black. A set of these items is called a Lenten array.

Lesser Feasts and Fasts: Book published by the Church Hymnal Corporation containing collects, lessons, Psalms, and brief biographical sketches for the minor saints' days and other observances found on the Prayer Book liturgical calendar.

Lessons: The biblical texts read at Morning and Evening Prayer and at the Eucharist. The Daily Offices call for one or two lessons and a selection from the Psalms; the Eucharist calls for three lessons and a selection from the Psalter.

When two lessons are read at the Offices, one is from the Old Testament and one from the New. The eucharistic lectionary calls for an Old Testament lesson, a New Testament lesson (or Epistle), and a reading from one of the Gospels. (During Eastertide, readings from the Acts of the Apostles may replace Old Testament readings.) All of the lessons except for the Gospel may be read by lay persons; the Gospel is read only by an ordained person. Reading the Gospel is, in fact, one of the distinctive actions of a deacon, if one is present.

Letter Dimissory: Letter from one bishop to another requesting that a priest or deacon be permitted to change the diocese in which he or she is canonically resident. Each ordained person is canonically resident in a diocese and under the jurisdiction of the bishop of that diocese; only in that diocese can the ordained person function sacramentally without getting special permission from the diocesan bishop. When an ordained person moves from one diocese to another, a change of canonical residence is usually in order.

Letter of Agreement: A document used by many Episcopal congregations to define their relationship with their clergy, including in it mutual expectations of the use of time, talent, finances, and, in some cases, the duration of the agreement.

Litany: A special form of intercessory prayer in which a deacon, priest, or cantor offers a series of petitions to which the people make a fixed response. The Great Litany (BCP, 148-55) is of special importance to Anglicans because it is Thomas Cranmer's first piece of liturgical writing prepared for use by the English in their native tongue. It represents the beginnings of the distinctive nature of Anglicanism because it was the first step toward the Book of Common Prayer. The Prayer Book also contains a litany for Ordinations (BCP, 548-51), and one at time of death (BCP, 462-64); it also uses a litany-like pattern for some of the intercessory prayers.

Liturgical Movement: A movement which began for Anglicans in the nineteenth century with the revival of very traditional forms of worship and ceremonial; a result of the Oxford Movement's concern to restore the centrality of the Eucharist to Anglican worship. This was controversial, but it had the positive effect of provoking serious study and thought about the role of worship in Christian life. In the twentieth century the ecumenical liturgical movement has produced a much clearer understanding of the Eucharist in the first centuries of the Christian era. This has been reflected in changes in church architecture, liturgies, and ceremonial which have brought to many a full sense of involvement and participation in the central act of Christian worship and identity formation. The liturgical movement emphasizes the centrality of the Eucharist in Christian life as an action in which everyone takes part and the need to make architecture, decoration, and ceremonial express this understanding of the Eucharist. Among the distinctive marks of the liturgical movement are the freestanding altar, the use of contemporary-language rites, the involvement of layfolk in the Eucharist, and a style of celebration which emphasizes clarity and straightforwardness.

Liturgics: Study of the texts, history, and theology of liturgies.

Liturgy: Word deriving from two Greek words meaning "work of the people"; the public prayer and worship of the people of God gathered in community; also, the texts of the rites that enable public worship to take place.

Liturgy of the Eucharist: The part of the eucharistic liturgy which begins with the Offertory, continues through the consecration and reception, and ends with the end of the rite itself. Called in the Prayer Book the Holy Communion (BCP, 333, 361).

Liturgy of the Word: The part of the eucharistic rite that begins with the reading of the lessons, continues through the sermon and the creed, and concludes with the confession and the peace. Called in BCP the Word of God (BCP, 323, 355).

Lord's Prayer: The prayer Jesus taught us to pray, which is part of almost every rite in the Prayer Book. It is now found in both the traditional translation and the one prepared by the International Council on English Texts (ICET) in contemporary language (BCP, 363-64). In the Eucharist, the Lord's Prayer comes at a very significant moment, immediately after the great "Amen" at the end of the Eucharistic Prayer, or Great Thanksgiving.

Lord's Supper: Traditional term for the Eucharist in the Anglican tradition; Cranmer called the rite in the first English Prayer Book (1549) "The Supper of the Lord." Later, however, the term *Holy Communion* became conventional usage and now *Eucharist* is coming to be the preferred term, as it lacks the controversial associations of other terms.

Lord's Table, The: The altar.

Low Mass: A celebration of the Eucharist in which the celebrant has no assisting ministers and only a single server. This form of ceremonial came into being only when the medieval church decided that all priests should celebrate the Mass daily rather than merely assist; previously the celebration with celebrant, deacon, and subdeacon had been the standard model. Nevertheless the "low" version of eucharistic ceremonial became the standard form after the Reformation for Catholic, Anglican, and Protestant traditions. The older High Mass form is, fortunately, now being recovered.

Low Sunday: The Sunday after Easter, so called because, after all the special services of Holy Week with their demand for extra sermons and other out-of-the-ordinary preparations, the Low Sunday mood is relaxed and restful. Seminarians often get to preach on Low Sunday to give the clergy a day off.

Lucenarium: The candle-lighting ceremony central to the Order of Worship for the Evening (BCP, 109-14).

M

Magnificat: Latin word meaning "magnifies" which starts the Latin version of the song of Mary as recorded in Luke's Gospel (1: 46-55). The traditional English version begins "My soul doth magnify the Lord." The text is used at Evening Prayer but may be used at Morning Prayer (BCP, 65, 119).

Maniple: Part of a set of eucharistic vestments, the maniple is a silk or linen band, usually in the seasonal color, traditionally worn by the celebrant on the left arm above the wrist. Probably deriving from a towel or handkerchief, the maniple is now rarely used because it can easily get in the celebrant's way.

Manual Acts: The actions done by the celebrant while reciting the Eucharistic Prayer. As specified by the Prayer Book these are, at a minimum, (1) to hold or place a hand on the bread while saying the words about Jesus' taking bread and giving thanks and breaking it and (2) to hold or place a hand on the cup and any other container of wine while saying the words about Jesus' taking the cup, giving thanks, and giving it to his disciples. These acts, according to the custom of the parish, may also include elevating the bread and wine and making the sign of the cross over them or holding the hands together over them. The sign of the cross is especially associated with the words "This is my body/blood" and with the *epiklesis,* or invocation of the Holy Spirit. Holding the hands together over the elements is especially associated with the *epiklesis*.

Figure 23. Priest Blessing
Married Couple

Marriage: The Prayer Book defines marriage as "a solemn and public covenant between a man and a woman in the presence of God" (BCP, 422). For an Episcopal priest or bishop to officiate at a wedding, at least one of the couple must be a baptized Christian, there must be at least two witnesses, and the marriage must conform to the laws of the state in which it takes place and to the Canons of the Church. The marriage rite is designed to take place in the context of a celebration of the Eucharist, although it can stand alone. Marriage in the Episcopal Church is a sacramental rite which conveys God's grace to enable the couple to keep the vows they make to each other and to the community. It is intended to be a lifelong union. Clergy are required to meet with the couple for a period of counseling prior to the service. Divorced persons may remarry in the Episcopal Church but only after the officiating priest has consulted with the bishop and received permission to perform the rite. For occasions in which the standard marriage rite (BCP, 423-32) does not seem appropriate, there is an Order for Marriage (BCP, 435-36) which allows for greater flexibility. In addition, there is a rite for the Blessing of a Civil Marriage (BCP, 433-34) and a rite for the renewal of wedding vows on the Anniversary of a Marriage (BOS, 144-46). [Figure 23]

Mass: Traditional name for the Eucharist, originating because the dismissal at the end of the Latin text of the Eucharist reads "Ite, missa est" ("Go; it is finished"). See also **high mass.**

Master of Ceremonies: A person, ordained or lay, whose role in the celebration of the Eucharist or other rite is to make sure that all the participants do what they are supposed to do when they are supposed to. The MC is in charge of ceremonial, the actions which bring the text of a liturgy to life. Thus, the MC, for example, reminds acolytes, if necessary, when to light candles, servers when to set up the altar, or the celebrant when to change vestments. The MC is a prompter, not required in parishes where the ceremonial is simple and the participants few, but invaluable when the service is elaborate and the participants many.

Matins, Mattins: Traditional word for the early morning office of the medieval monastic day, the term is now occasionally applied to the first of the two Anglican Daily Offices as an alternative name for Morning Prayer.

Maundy Thursday: Thursday of Holy Week, on which the church remembers Christ's institution of the Eucharist (BCP, 274-75) and, in some places, observes the ceremony of the washing of feet in remembrance of our Lord's washing the feet of his disciples. The name *Maundy* is a shortened form either of the word *commandment* in its early spelling *commaundement* or of the Latin words *mandatum novum,* which means "new commandment"; the Gospel associated with this day is of Jesus' saying to his disciples, "I give you a new commandment: Love one another as I have loved you." Because of the distinctive footwashing ceremony of Maundy Thursday, that part of the service is referred to in some places as the "Maundy."

Member, Membership: Because the church is both the Body of Christ and a very human institution which has to care about membership numbers, the definition of what makes one a member of the Episcopal Church has recently undergone change. At one time, only those who had been confirmed by an Episcopal bishop could receive communion. Those who had been baptized as Episcopalians were members of the church but were not communicants until they were confirmed. Those baptized in non-Episcopal churches were considered Christians but not Episcopalians until they were confirmed by an Episcopal bishop (or received into the Episcopal Church by a bishop if they had been confirmed in the Roman Catholic or Orthodox Churches). Recently, however, we have recovered the full implications of Baptism as the full rite of initiation into the Body of Christ. The institutional consequences of this are still being worked out, and consultation with the rector or vicar is recommended. At the moment, however, a *member* of the Episcopal Church is one who has been baptized by water in the name of the Father and of the Son and of the Holy Spirit in the Episcopal Church or in another Christian church and whose Baptism has been duly recorded in the Episcopal Church. An *adult member* is a member sixteen years of age or older. The Episcopal Church also expects that its adult members will have made, after appropriate instruction, a mature public affirmation of faith and commitment to the responsibilities and promises made by or for them at Baptism and have been confirmed or received by a bishop of the Episcopal Church or a church in communion with the Episcopal Church (such as another member church of the Anglican communion). Members who have received Holy Communion at least three times in the past year are also considered *communicants.* See **communicant.**

Mensa: The top of an altar.

Minister: From a Latin word meaning "a servant"; anyone who ministers to the needs of others, including one who leads worship; thus the more conventional meaning in Protestant circles of an ordained person. But the Episcopal Church also affirms that all Christians are called to ministry at Baptism and only some are called to ordained ministries. Thus all Christians are ministers, through whom, according to the Catechism, the "Church carries out its mission." The Catechism defines the ministers of the church as "lay persons, bishops, priests, and deacons," and spells out in detail the ministries of each (BCP, 855-56). In fact, layfolk licensed by the bishop can conduct public worship according to directions laid down by the Prayer Book (BCP, 36, 74), which calls the worship leader of the Daily Offices an officiant specifically to avoid distinguishing between ordained and lay ministers.

Ministers: Celebrant, assisting clergy, and all others (ordained or lay) who help at the altar during the celebration of the Eucharist. In the Episcopal tradition the term does not necessarily mean an ordained person.

Ministration to the Sick: Rite in the Prayer Book (BCP, 453-61) which includes readings from Scripture, prayer, the Laying on of Hands and Anointing, and the Eucharist. Special prayers which can be used by someone who is sick are also found in this rite.

Ministration at the Time of Death: Rite in the Prayer Book (BCP, 462-67) including a prayer for one near death, a Litany at the Time of Death, a text for a vigil prior to a funeral, and prayers for use when the body of the deceased is brought to the church.

Ministry: The Catechism calls ministry the means through which the church carries out its mission, which is "to restore all people to unity with God and each other in Christ." It also defines those with a ministry in the church as "all its members," ordained and lay. In brief, the ministry of the laity is to represent and bear witness to Christ and his church, to carry on Christ's reconciling work in the world, and to take their place in the life, worship, and governance of the church. The Catechism also spells out the ministries of bishops, priests, and deacons (BCP, 855-56) and concludes by defining the duty of all Christians as "to follow Christ; to come together week by week for corporate worship; and to work, pray, and give for the spread of the kingdom of God."

Missal: Traditional term for altar book, the large book containing the texts needed to celebrate the Eucharist used at the altar.

Missal Stand: Metal or wooden stand or pillow used to support the altar book or missal if one is used for the purpose of celebrating the Eucharist.

Mission: A word with two distinct meanings. (1) The mission of the church, as defined by the Catechism, is "to restore all people to unity with God and each other in Christ" by praying, worshiping, proclaiming the gospel, and promoting justice, peace, and love (BCP, 855). This is the task of all members, ordained and lay. (2) A mission is a worshiping unit of the church which is to some extent financially dependent on the diocese and is thus not a parish, which is by definition self-supporting. The rector of a mission is, technically, the bishop of the diocese; the bishop appoints the priest-in-charge, who may be called the vicar. One form of support the diocese may provide is money to support the operation of the mission. Becoming a mission and eventually becoming self-supporting and achieving parish status is the customary way in which a new congregation becomes part of the church. The admission of a new congregation into union with the diocese requires an act of a diocesan convention.

Mission Committee: In some dioceses called the bishop's advisory committee, BAC, or bishop's committee, the "vestry" of a mission, selected either by the bishop or by a vote of the congregation of the mission. This governing body differs from a vestry in that a vestry hires the rector with the advice and consent of the bishop, while a mission committee, although it may recommend a name of someone to the bishop to become the vicar, must abide by the decision of the bishop as to whom the vicar will be.

Missionary: One chosen and supported to carry out the mission of the church in other lands or in regions or social groups in the United States not otherwise reached by the regular structures of the church. The Episcopal Church has authorized missionaries in over thirty-two foreign countries; it also recognizes the missionary activities at home and abroad of a number of agencies, including the National Institute for Lay Training and the Church Army.

Mitre: The liturgical headgear and part of the insignia of a bishop; a shield-shaped hat made of satin with two fringed ribbons hanging down from the back. Bishops wear their mitres in procession and when pronouncing episcopal blessings.

Monastery: The house of a religious community, although conventionally the residence of a male religious community, as opposed to a convent, the house of a female religious community.

Monk: A member of a male religious order who has taken vows of poverty, chastity, and obedience.

Monasticism: The style of Christian life characterized by the pursuit of personal sanctification through work and prayer and adherence to the three monastic vows of poverty, chastity, and obedience to a superior in a common life. Monastic life centers around recitation of the Offices and daily Eucharist. Monasticism was virtually eliminated from the Anglican tradition at the time of the Reformation in the sixteenth century, although the appearance of enterprises like the community at Little Gidding organized by Nicholas Ferrar in the seventeenth century suggests that the monastic ideal was still alive, albeit in less traditional forms. The full revival of monasticism in Anglicanism took place in the nineteenth century in England and soon spread to the Episcopal Church. There are now over thirty-two religious orders for men and women listed in the *Episcopal Church Annual*; among the most widely-known are the Society of St. John the Evangelist, the Order of the Holy Cross, the Order of St. Benedict, the Order of St. Anne, the Order of St. Helena, and the Society of St. Margaret.

Monstrance: Frame, usually in gold or silver, used to display the eucharistic bread for veneration, as in the service of benediction of the blessed sacrament. Now rarely seen, except in parishes in which the service of benediction is part of the liturgical tradition.

Morning Prayer: Also known as matins, the first of the two Daily Offices created by Archbishop Cranmer out of the eight monastic hours for the Prayer Book of 1549. Morning Prayer consists of Opening Sentences, an optional Confession and Absolution, recitation of Psalms, readings from Scripture according to the Daily Office lectionary with Canticles, the Apostles' Creed, Suffrages, and Prayers (BCP, 37-60, 75-102). With Evening Prayer, it forms the basis of Anglican spirituality.

Movable Feast: A feast on the liturgical calendar that does not occur on the same day each year. The most important is Easter, which may be on any day between March 23 and April 25. The date of Easter determines Ash Wednesday (forty weekdays before), Ascension Day (forty days after), Pentecost (fifty days after), and thus the length of the Epiphany and Pentecost seasons. Because Advent must have four Sundays, the actual Sunday on which it starts is determined by the day of the week on which the immovable feast of Christmas falls.

N

Narthex: In a traditionally arranged church, a room or space between the main door to the outside and the main door to the nave; in the narthex those coming to worship may gather to remove coats or chat with each other.

Nave: In a traditionally arranged church, the large room between the narthex and the chancel or choir. Historically, when the Gothic church was developed, the nave was the church of the laity and had its own altars, while the chancel was the church of the clergy and monastics. At the time of the Reformation, the nave altars were taken out, and the one altar of the chancel was to function as the altar for all the people. Chancel screens, which almost completely shut off the chancel from the nave, reinforcing the idea of two separate rooms, were taken down. This was a stopgap measure —it brought clergy and laity closer together, but did not bring people closer to the altar. Before a better solution could be worked out, the temporary measure became what people expected, and the gothic model for church architecture as we know it was established. [Plate C]

New Fire: Lighted at the beginning of the Great Vigil of Easter (BCP, 285), the new fire is the source of the flame used to light the Paschal candle.

New Testament: The canonical books of the Bible whose authority is recognized by the Christian church but not by Judaism, with which we share what Christians call the Old

Testament. The New Testament provides two readings at the Eucharist and at the Daily Office, one from the Gospels and one from the Epistles.

Nicene Creed: Creed used in the Eucharist (BCP, 326-28, 358-59) that is, with the Apostles' Creed, the definitive statement of Christian faith, according to the Lambeth Quadrilateral. It takes its name from the origin of part of its text at the Council of Nicea in A.D. 325. This creed developed out of the baptismal affirmations of those uniting with the Christian community and establishes the framework for the continuing reflection of the church on the simultaneous humanity and divinity of Christ. The creed evolved from that statement of Nicea into a full affirmation of the faith of the church by around A.D. 450. In Rite One, there are two texts of the Nicene Creed. The first is a new and more accurate translation prepared by the International Consultation on English Texts and is the only text in Rite Two. The second is the translation used in the Prayer Book since Cranmer. The Nicene Creed is used as the definitive statement of the faith throughout Christendom, except that the version used in Eastern churches says that the Spirit "proceeds from the Father" while the version used in the West reads, as in the Prayer Book, "from the Father and the Son." This is the famous "filioque" clause over which the Eastern and Western Churches parted ways in A.D. 1054.

Noonday Prayer: Short title for An Order of Service for Noonday (BCP, 103-07), a modern version of the ancient service of None. The service consists of an opening versicle and response, selections from the Psalter, a brief reading from Scripture, and prayers, including the Lord's Prayer. This service, along with An Order of Worship for the Evening (BCP, 108-14; often called vespers) and An Order for Compline (BCP, 127-35), now makes it possible for individuals and parishes to mark more of the hours of the day with corporate prayer, and for Episcopal monastic communities to observe a four- or five-hour Office from the Prayer Book.

Novice: A probationary member of a religious community who wears the habit and takes part in the corporate life but who has not made a life profession, or taken the final vows. This probationary period is designed to allow someone to explore the religious life and then, if he or she does not feel called to a life profession, to withdraw without feeling that he or she has broken a commitment.

Nun: Member of a religious order of women living under vows of poverty, chastity, and obedience. Among the orders of nuns in the Episcopal Church are the Order of St. Anne, the Society of St. Margaret, and the Order of St. Helena.

Nunc Dimittis: Latin for "Now let depart," the first words of the Song of Simeon (Luke 2:29-32). This text appears as an optional Canticle in Morning Prayer (BCP, 51-52, 93) and Evening Prayer (BCP, 66, 120), although it is traditionally associated with Evening Prayer.

Nuptual Eucharist, Nuptual Mass: Eucharist celebrated at a wedding, as provided for by the Prayer Book (BCP, 432).

O

Oblations: Term meaning "offering" used for the bread and wine offered for consecration at the Eucharist to distinguish them from the alms, or money-offering, as in the Offertory sentence "Let us with gladness present the alms and oblations of our life and labor to the Lord" (BCP, 344, 377).

Occasional Offices: Those Prayer Book rites which are done only when the occasion is appropriate, such as Baptism and Ministration to the Sick, as opposed to rites such as the Eucharist, which it is always appropriate to do (except on Good Friday and Holy Saturday).

Offertory: The offering of the bread and wine, along with the money offering and other gifts, is a fundamental part of the eucharistic action. The Prayer Book requires that these be presented to the celebrant at the altar by "representatives of the congregation" (BCP, 333, 361).

Offertory Procession: The Prayer Book requires (BCP, 333, 361) that the offering of bread and wine, money, and other gifts be brought to the celebrant or deacon at the altar by "representatives of the congregation." This can be made into an elaborate moment in the ceremonial if the procession of the alms and oblations is accompanied by acolytes and perhaps a thurifer bearing incense. It can also be very significant to the members of the congregation who actually carry the bread and wine, especially if one of them has baked the bread. The Prayer Book contains many options about the performing of its rites; an Offertory procession is not optional but an essential part of the eucharistic rites.

Offertory Sentences: Passages of Scripture which may be said or sung to signal the beginning of the Offertory (see BCP, 343-44, 376-77).

Oil: Oil is used in the church in two forms: (1) chrism, blessed by a bishop and used in Baptism (BCP, 307), and (2) oil of unction, blessed by a bishop or priest and used in services of healing or ministry to the sick (BCP, 455-56; BOS, 151).

Oil Stock: Small container, usually of silver and decorated with a cross, used to carry and store the oil of chrism or unction.

Old Testament: The collection of canonical books which the Christian church shares with Judaism. The first lesson at the Eucharist is taken from the Old Testament, as is the first lesson of the three provided for each day's reading of the Daily Office. Some books of the Old Testament which became part of the Bible of the medieval church were not included in the Bible of Judaism; at the time of the Reformation in England, these books were put together in a separate section between the Old and New Testaments and called by the special name Apocrypha. This group includes Ecclesiasticus, the Wisdom of Solomon, Tobias, Maccabees, and others. Selections from these books are read in the Episcopal Church; the apocryphal books are considered authoritative for moral instruction but not for doctrinal matters.

Orans Position: Position assumed by the celebrant during various prayers of the Eucharist, including collects and the Eucharistic Prayer. The hands are held shoulder high, palms upward, and elbows slightly bent. The name is a

form of the Latin word *orare,* which means "to pray for."
[Figure 23a]

Figure 23a.   Orans Position

Order: The Prayer Book contains Orders for the Eucharist,
Marriage, and Burial which provide the essentials for performing these rites when the situation makes the full rites
inappropriate (BCP, 400-05, 435-36, 506-07).

Orders, Holy: The three offices to which one may be
ordained—bishops, priests, and deacons.

Orders, Religious: Groups or congregations who live under a
special rule, usually created by their founder, involving vows
of poverty, chastity, and obedience. Members devote themselves to a life of work and prayer organized around the
Offices of the Hours and daily Eucharist. The medieval
orders were abolished at the time of the Reformation in
England and were revived in the nineteenth century. The
more than thirty-one religious orders in the Episcopal
Church include the Society of St. John the Evangelist (also
known as the Cowley Fathers), the Brotherhood of St. Gregory, the Society of St. Francis, and the Order of the Holy
Cross for men; and the Society of St. Margaret, the Order of
St. Anne, and the Order of St. Helena for women. Recently,

some nontraditional religious orders have appeared, retaining the fundamental concept of a common devotional life and mission but involving both married and celibate people, and both men and women. Among the orders in the Episcopal Church which in one way or another embody creative variations on the standard monastic model are the Worker Brothers of the Holy Spirit (married and celibate men), the Worker Sisters of the Holy Spirit (married and celibate women), and the Order of Agape and Reconciliation (men and women, married and celibate).

Ordinal: The text of the rites of Ordination, taken together. It has its own name because at one time it was published as a separate book. Now, however, the rites for Ordination of bishops, priests, and deacons are found on pages 511-55 of the *Prayer Book*.

Ordinand: One being ordained at a service of Ordination.

Ordinary: The bishop of a diocese, who has the final word in the ordering of what is taught and what rites are celebrated in the parishes of his diocese. When an episcopate is vacant, the Standing Committee of a diocese is the ordinary. The word is also used for the texts of the Eucharist or the Daily Offices which remain the same or change only slightly, as opposed to the Propers of those rites, which change according to the ecclesiastical day or season.

Ordination: Rite by which one becomes a deacon (BCP, 537-47), priest (BCP, 525-35), or bishop (BCP, 512-23). In each case, the ordinand is presented to the ordaining bishop (in the case of ordination to the episcopate, the Presiding Bishop or a bishop appointed by the Presiding Bishop) by lay and clergy presenters who certify publicly that he or she has been appropriately chosen. The ordinand then declares loyalty to the church and its doctrine, discipline, and worship, and the congregation expresses its desire that the ordinand be ordained and pledges to uphold him or her in this ministry. There follows the Litany for Ordinations (BCP, 548-51), the lessons appointed, and the sermon. After the Creed and public examination about the ordinant's willingness to take on the special purposes of the office, a hymn invoking the presence of the Holy Spirit is sung. At this point, things vary a bit. If the ordination is to the diaconate, the bishop lays his hands on the ordinand; if it is to the priesthood, he is joined in the laying on of hands by priests. If the ordination is to the office of bishop, then the Presiding Bishop and at least two other bishops place their hands on the ordinand's head. Following this, the ordinand is vested according to the order—a stole over the left shoulder and tied under the right arm for a deacon, a stole and chasuble for a priest, and a mitre, pastoral staff, and ring for a bishop. The ordinand is then presented with a Bible and leads in the Peace. Later, the newly ordained is given the chance to function at the Eucharist in keeping with the nature of the office.

Ornaments, Church: The furnishings and liturgical furniture of a church building; the Book of Occasional Services contains a rite for the blessing of such ornaments (BOS, 177-94).

Orphreys: Bands of contrasting material used to adorn chasubles, frequently consisting of a single stripe running from the neckband to the hem on the front and back, often combined with a "V" running from the shoulders to a point on the vertical stripe about one-third of the way down.

P

Pall: Word with two meanings in the church: (1) the cloth placed over the casket during a funeral instead of flowers, the American flag, or other decoration, and (2) the stiff white linen-covered board which is placed over the chalice to support the burse and chalice veil. [Figure 24]

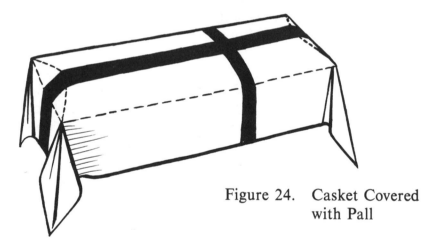

Figure 24. Casket Covered with Pall

Palm Sunday: The last Sunday in Lent and the day on which Holy Week begins. The day commemorates Jesus' triumphant procession into Jerusalem and is marked by a blessing of palms and a procession (BCP, 270-72), usually with the singing of the hymn "All glory, laud, and honor to thee, Redeemer King" or other suitable hymn or anthem. The day is also marked by the reading of the passion Gospel from Matthew, Mark, or Luke.

Palms: Leaves of the palm tree which are blessed and carried in procession on Palm Sunday. In some places, palms blessed on Palm Sunday are retained and burned to provide ashes for the next year's observance of Ash Wednesday.

Parish: A parish must be thought of in two ways. Both are necessary, but sometimes they work at cross purposes. In either case, a parish is a local manifestation of something larger. First, it is a worshiping community of Christians who gather weekly at Christ's altar to experience his redemptive love through celebrating the Eucharist and who then further his redemptive work in the world. Here the lives of its members are brought before God and each other in sacramental process from Baptism to burial, nurtured by table fellowship with Christ and each other. In this regard, the parish is a specific and local manifestation of the church as the risen body of Christ. Second, it is the local administrative unit of the diocese. It is self-supporting and is governed by a vestry composed of lay members of the congregation elected at the annual parish meeting. The vestry hires the rector, who is the chief liturgical and sacramental officer of the parish and functions as the celebrant or officiant at worship and also works to enable all members of the congregation to find and live out their different vocations. The rector may be assisted by other clergy. The rector may nominate from among the vestry a senior warden who is elected by the vestry or congregation to be the official spokesperson for the vestry. The vestry may also elect a junior warden to be responsible for maintenance. The vestry's job includes responsibility for all parish activities, including planning budgets, running canvass or fund-raising activities, deciding how money will be spent, approving plans for program, education, and outreach, and often choosing delegates to the diocesan convention. These organizational and administrative functions are necessary if the more primary community-oriented and sacramental work of the parish is to get done, but they from time to time obscure what is more important. On the other hand, the experience of the community can also inform the administrative and organizational aspects of parish life. When that happens, the two can reinforce each other positively, because the administrative side of parish life can be a place where people learn how to live out the Gospel in their lives, which are more like administration than they are like worship. In this case, "to administrate" can mean "to minister to."

Parish House: The part of the physical plant of a church which often contains offices, meeting rooms, and other facilities, so called to distinguish it from the sanctuary area, which contains the centrum or eucharistic room.

Parish Meeting: Each parish is required to have an annual parish meeting at which the vestry reports to the congregation on the state of the parish and new members of the vestry are elected.

Parish Profile: Document which may be prepared when a parish is without a rector and must search for another. The purpose of the parish profile is to help the parish and those whom it considers hiring to understand the parish. Each congregation has a unique history, style, and understanding of its mission; to help it find the rector best for it, the parish often hires a consultant who works with the members to help them write a description of its self-understanding, its goals, its personality, its organization, and its peculiar needs for clerical leadership. This document is the parish profile.

Parish Register: Each parish is required to keep records of Baptisms, Confirmations, Marriages, transfers of membership, and burials. All acts like Baptisms, Confirmations, and Marriages must be witnessed by several people, whose signatures go into the Parish Register, making it a legal resource for establishing personal identity.

Parochial: Having to do with a parish; thus, the parochial report is a report submitted annually by a parish, listing the numbers and kinds of services performed during the year.

Parson: Word for the clergy, from the word *person*; in the Middle Ages the rector of a parish held legal title to parish property and was thus the legal "person" one had to deal with in regard to parish business. Now it is rarely used but can mean any parish priest. It can still have significance beyond nostalgia in small towns where the Episcopal priest has a certain authority in the community outside the parish.

Pascha Nostrum: Latin for "our passover," the name of the versicle and response which may be said by the celebrant and congregation after the Breaking of the Bread—"Christ our Passover is sacrificed for us; Therefore let us keep the Feast," with "Alleluia" before and after in Easter Season and at other times optionally, except in Lent—during the Eucharist (BCP, 337, 364).

Figure 25.   Paschal Candle

Paschal Candle: Large white candle often but not necessarily decorated with a cross, the Greek letters alpha and omega, the year, grains of incense, and other symbols of the resurrection. It is lighted from the new fire at the Great

Vigil of Easter and is carried into the church, most appropriately by a deacon, who then sings the Exsultet. The Paschal candle burns at all services during the Easter season. It may be lighted for Baptisms at other times during the church year, and a baptismal candle may be lighted from it and presented to the newly baptized. The Paschal candle may also be carried in procession and placed near the casket or urn during the Burial of the Dead. The Paschal candle represents for us the "light of Christ," words proclaimed three times by the one carrying it into the church at the Easter Vigil; it is one of the great symbols of our Easter hope. [Figure 25]

Paschal Candlestand: Stand of sufficient size to hold the Paschal candle and display it prominently.

Paschal Vigil: Another name for The Easter Vigil; the word *paschal* derives from the Hebrew word for Passover, the festival that provided the background for Jesus' crucifixion and resurrection, according to the synoptic Gospels. John's Gospel names Jesus as the true Paschal lamb. The celebrant's address to the congregation at the start of the Easter Vigil proclaims this "the Passover of the Lord" (BCP, 285).

Passion Sunday: The Sunday before Easter, or Palm Sunday, so named because it begins the observance of Passiontide, or Holy Week, and includes the first reading of the Gospel narrative of Jesus' crucifixion. *Passion* here means "suffering" rather than "enthusiasm."

Pastor: Word for the clergy deriving from a Latin word for shepherd. To call a member of the clergy a pastor is to recall one aspect of the priestly role, that of caring, protective responsibility. As a word for part of the role of ordained persons, it is especially appropriate for bishops, since they are ordained to "feed and tend the flock of Christ," who is the good shepherd. But priests, too, are ordained to be "faithful pastors."

Pastoral Letter: Public letter from a bishop to all members of a diocese; also, a public letter from the House of Bishops written during its meetings and required to be read or otherwise promulgated (made known) to all members of the church as soon as possible.

Pastoral Ministry: Pastoral and prophetic ministries are often contrasted, although they are better seen as complementary. A pastoral ministry proclaims God's reconciling love to the community through care for the sick, the grieving, the needy, and those in pain, while a prophetic ministry calls the people of God to minister to the homeless, the weak, and the afflicted and to promote justice, freedom, and peace.

Pastoral Offices: Section of rites in the Prayer Book (BCP, 411-507) which enable members of the church to enact significant moments in their lives in the presence of and with the assistance of the entire community. These rites include Confirmation, Marriage, Thanksgiving for a Child, Reconciliation of a Penitent, Ministration to the Sick, and the Burial of the Dead.

Pastoral Staff: The bishop's crosier; a reminder that the bishop is the shepherd of his diocese.

Figure 26.

Chalice with Purificator, Paten, Burse, and Veil

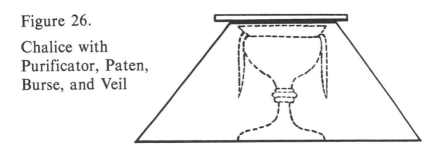

Paten: A shallow dish, usually of gold or silver, used to hold the eucharistic bread during the consecration and administration, when it is in the form of unleavened wafers. The paten often carries the priest's host to the altar as it rides on top of the chalice and under the pall in the "stack," along with the chalice veil and the burse. With the increased use of real loaves of bread in the Eucharist, the paten may be supplemented by bread trays, baskets, bowls, or plates or dispensed with altogether. [Figure 26]

Pater Noster: Latin for "Our Father," the opening words of the Lord's Prayer, found in almost every rite in the Prayer Book.

Patristics: From the Latin word for "father"; the study of the first 500 to 800 years of the church's history, also known as the age of the church fathers. Since the churches of the Anglican communion have always looked back to the patristic period as a time in the history of Christianity we can use as a model, it is appropriate that many Anglican scholars devote themselves to the study of patristics.

Patronal Feast: Feast of the patron of a parish or other religious organization such as a school or religious order, i.e., the saint for which it is named. This can be a time of great community celebration. Usually held on the feast day of that saint, the observance can be transferred to the following Sunday to enable more to attend, unless it falls in the seasons of Advent, Lent, or Easter, the Sundays of which take precedence over everything else.

Peace: Ancient sacramental greeting of the faithful in the Eucharist, a sign of love and union in Christ. In the Prayer Book, it comes after the Confession (BCP, 332, 360), but may also take place at the time of administration of the bread and wine. The celebrant and the congregation first exchange the wish that the peace of the Lord be always with them, and then members of the congregation greet each other individually in the name of the Lord. This may be done ritually with a handshake, handclasp, or embrace. [Figure 27]

Figure 27.   Exchanging the Peace

Pectoral Cross: Cross of silver or gold hanging from a chain around the neck to a spot on the breast, at the location of the pectoral muscles. An especially fine pectoral cross, often adorned with jewels, is part of the official regalia of bishops, although other clergy often wear more modest versions.

Penance: Traditional name for the rite for the Reconciliation of a Penitent (BCP, 447-52), which appears in two forms. Form One is shorter, and contains the essential Blessing, Confession, Absolution, and Dismissal. Form Two includes these, but adds sentences of Scripture, an Examination, and a Laying on of Hands, and is perhaps more appropriate for marking a major turning-point in the life of the penitent. The name *penance* derives from the fact that in the past the absolution was made conditional on the penitent's performing acts of penance.

Penitent: One who feels separated from the Christian community as a result of his or her conduct and seeks through reconciliation to overcome that distance through a sacramental act of Confession and Absolution.

Penitential Order: For each of the eucharistic rites in the Prayer Book there is a Penitential Order (BCP, 319-21, 351-53) consisting of an Acclamation, Confession, Absolution, and options for use of the Decalogue, sentences from Scripture, or other resources. The Penitential Order can be used at the beginning of either Eucharist, in which case the Confession after the Intercessions is not used; or it can be used on its own.

Pentecost: The Sunday fifty days after Easter on which the church remembers the bestowal of the gift of the Holy Spirit on the apostles (Acts 2:1). The name derives from the Greek name of the Jewish Festival of Weeks fifty days after Passover, when the event originally occurred. Because this event signaled the beginning of the apostles' public proclamation of Jesus as the Christ, it is often called the birthday of the Christian church. Because it is also a traditional day for Baptisms, and because people at one time uniformly wore white garments in which to be baptized, the day also became known as Whitsunday (White Sunday). Now the color of the day is red, followed by white for Trinity Sunday; the rest of the season is green, except that in some places the Last Sunday after Pentecost is red or white.

Pentecost, Season of: The season of the church year which runs from the Sunday of Pentecost until the First Sunday of Advent; in this season, Sundays are numbered after Pentecost. The cycle of the liturgical year from Advent through Easter recalls Jesus' earthly ministry, culminating in the remembrance of his death, resurrection, and postresurrection appearances. The Pentecost season calls us to explore the significance of the church itself as the sign of Christ's continued presence and ongoing activity in the world. The liturgical color is green.

Petition: A section of one of the intercessory prayers, or Prayers of the People, which are organized so that each section deals with a specific area of the church's concerns

(BCP, 328-29, 383-93), including the church itself, the nation and the world, the concerns of the local community, those who suffer or are in trouble, and the departed. The role of intercessory prayer is to hold the world in all its brokenness and neediness before God, the source of reconciliation and healing. These Prayers of the People are arranged so that members of the congregation can make their personal concerns part of the prayers of the whole church by adding specific petitions to the general ones voiced by the reader.

Pew: Long, bench-like seat used for congregational seating in traditionally arranged church buildings. Recently designed churches often use chairs instead of pews because pews are hard to move around and limit the flexibility of the worship space.

Phos Hilaron: Greek for "O gracious light"; the hymn that appears in the Order of Worship for Evening to be sung or said following the lighting of the vesper candle (BCP, 112).

Piscina: From a Latin word for "basin"; a small sink, usually found in the sacristy, whose drain goes directly into the ground. It is used to dispose of water left over after Baptisms or after cleaning the chalice and paten following a celebration of the Eucharist and, in some places, consecrated wine not consumed during the Eucharist.

Plainsong: Medieval music for singing the services of the church, also known as Gregorian chant because of a tradition that Pope Gregory the Great (d. 604) played a major role in its development. Plainsong is modal music sung by a choir in unison; its effects are among the most haunting in sacred music. The *Hymnal* contains a number of hymns and settings of the eucharistic and Daily Office texts in plainsong.

Postcommunion Prayer: The prayer of thanksgiving for the Eucharist and for support from God in "the work you have given us to do" which follows reception of the bread and wine in the Eucharist (BCP, 339, 365-66).

Postulant: One who has reached the stage of postulancy in the process toward Holy Orders or toward admission into a religious order. Someone seeking Holy Orders first meets with his or her home rector and vestry and, with their positive recommendation, with the bishop of the diocese. If the bishop requests, the person then has a physical examination and a psychological evaluation and meets with the diocesan Commission on Ministry. The COM may ask the person to do a year's internship in a parish setting under the supervision of the rector. At some point, the COM will recommend to the bishop whether or not the person should be named a postulant. With all this advice and counsel in hand, the bishop decides whether or not to name the person a postulant. If the person is so named, he or she then enters a seminary or begins some other appropriate educational process. If all goes well, in a year and a half to two years, the postulant will advance in the process and become a candidate for Holy Orders.

Prayer Book: A familiar way of referring to the Book of Common Prayer.

Prayer Desk: Piece of church furniture which may be built into a choir stall or left freestanding. It consists of a shelf on top to support a Prayer Book, a storage shelf underneath for a hymnal or other books, and a kneeler at the bottom which usually can be folded out of the way when not needed. [Figure 28]

Prayers of the People: Another term for the intercessions, the great prayer for "Christ's Church and the world" (BCP, 328-30, 383-93), which is appropriately read by a deacon or lay reader. Here, the congregation offers up our world and our lives in all their brokenness to the one from whom come all healing and reconciliation. In each of the forms provided in the Prayer Book, there is opportunity for members of the congregation to ask that their own special concerns become part of the prayer of the whole church. The content of the model intercessions reminds us that the concerns of the church include individual and local suffering and loss but also larger concerns for justice and peace.

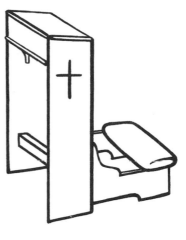

Figure 28.   Prayer Desk,
                     or Prie Dieu

Preacher, Preaching: The Prayer Book calls for a sermon to be delivered at every celebration of the Eucharist and at every performance of the rites intended to function as the Liturgy of the Word in a celebration of the Eucharist, such as Baptism, Marriage, Burial, Confirmation, and Ordination. It also permits a sermon to occur during or at the end of one of the Offices. Preaching in the Episcopal Church is thus primarily liturgical preaching, taking place in a liturgical context and not functioning as an end in itself. One of the major functions it serves is to bring the lessons appointed for the occasion to bear on that occasion. Episcopal preachers are, for the most part, not free to choose any text that suits them. They must accept the discipline of the liturgical lectionary and the biblical readings it provides. They must, as part of their sermon, perform the interpretive task of making clear what the lessons meant in their original context and exploring what they could mean for the people gathered to hear them again in the present.

Preaching Gown: A long black garment with bell-shaped sleeves, often with velvet bands similar to an academic gown, worn with a cassock and preaching tabs when the wearer's only role in a service is to preach.

Preaching Scarf: Another name for a tippet.

Preaching Tabs: White starched neckwear in the shape of an inverted V worn with a cassock by a designated preacher who is not the celebrant; also called preaching bands. They may also be part of the garb of a bishop when wearing rochet and chimere.

Preface: The introductory part of the Great Thanksgiving, from the salutation through the Sanctus. Variable Proper Prefaces for the Lord's Day, the liturgical seasons, and other special occasions are provided (BCP, 344-49, 377-82) for use in the Eucharistic Prayers which anticipate their use. Thus, Eucharistic Prayers A and B in Rite Two provide for the use of a Proper Preface, while Eucharistic Prayers C and D do not.

Prelate: A bishop, although the term is now rarely heard.

President: In some places, the celebrant is called the president of the eucharistic assembly.

President's Chair: If the celebrant is called the president, then his or her chair is called the president's chair.

Presiding Bishop: The presiding officer of the Episcopal Church, elected at a meeting of the General Convention by the House of Bishops with the concurrence of the House of Deputies for a term of office to end at the General Convention nearest his sixty-eighth birthday. The Presiding Bishop has his office at 815 Second Avenue in New York City, the national headquarters of the Episcopal Church. The Presiding Bishop has no cathedral, but does have a throne in the Cathedral of St. Peter and St. Paul in Washington, D.C. The responsibilities of the Presiding Bishop are to preside at meetings of the House of Bishops and of the Executive Council, to be the chief officiant at ordinations of bishops, to oversee the entire program of the church, and to represent the Episcopal Church on a large number of boards and committees and in relationships with other member churches of the Anglican communion and religious traditions different from ours. The Presiding Bishop is a symbol of the unity of all the dioceses of the Episcopal Church.

Presiding Bishop's Fund for World Relief: A fund to which anyone may contribute which is used by the Presiding Bishop to provide global short-term emergency relief.

Prie-dieu: French for "pray God"; another term for a prayer desk. [Figure 28]

Priest: Traditional translation of the Greek *presbyteros.* One of the four orders of ministry in the Episcopal Church, the priest is ordained to "represent Christ and his Church, particularly as a pastor to the people; to share with the bishop in the overseeing of the Church; to proclaim the Gospel; to administer the sacraments; and to bless and declare pardon in the name of God" (BCP, 856). This means that the priest is authorized to be the celebrant at the Eucharist, to baptize when the bishop is not present, and to pronounce absolution of sins to the penitent. The priest also is trained in pastoral care and the conduct of public worship and is authorized to preach; because of the nature of this office, most priests are rectors of parishes. Other priests exercise their vocation in settings other than the parish. Some are chaplains; others find their ministry in activities not supported financially by the church. These latter are called nonstipendiary priests. The sign of the priestly office is the stole, worn around the neck allowing the ends to hang straight down the front of the priest's body (as opposed to the deacon's manner of wearing the stole across the left shoulder and tied under the right arm). Priests may wear the chasuble while celebrating the Eucharist, while deacons may wear the dalmatic. The role of the priest is to enable the people of God to be what they are called to be. To that end, the priest convenes the eucharistic assembly and in the larger exercise of the office enables the members of Christ's body to discover and live out their vocations. The title of the priest is "The Reverend," or "The Rev.," not "Rev." A man who is a priest is in some places referred to as "Father"; a woman who is a priest is in some places called "Mother."

Primate: Title used in some member churches of the Anglican communion for the chief bishop in that church; thus, the Archbishop of Canterbury is the "Primate of all England" (for complex historical reasons, the Archbishop of York is the "Primate of England"), and the Archbishop of Sydney is the "Primate of the Church of England in Australia." Our Presiding Bishop is the "Primate of the Episcopal Church in the United States of America," but he has the title Presiding Bishop rather than Archbishop.

Prior: One of the titles given to a man who heads a monastic religious house. Among the religious orders in the Episcopal Church, the Oratory of the Good Shepherd is headed by a prior.

Prioress: One of the titles given to a woman who heads a monastic religious house. The Order of Agape and Reconciliation is headed by a prioress.

Priory: One of the names that can be given to a house occupied by a religious community. Among the religious orders in the Episcopal Church, the Order of the Holy Cross and the Congregation of Our Lady of Mount Carmel have priories.

Procession: Formal walk of ministers, servers, acolytes, and sometimes members of the congregation. Usually a service begins with a procession into the church ending at the altar. On major feast days, the procession may gather at the altar rather than at the back of the church and make a solemn procession down the main aisle, around the side aisles, and back up the main aisle. On some or all of the Sundays in Advent and Lent, the Great Litany may be sung or said in procession. On Palm Sunday, the Prayer Book provides that the entire congregation gather at a place other than the church building so that the palms may be blessed and the procession into the church include everyone. Processions may use incense, torches, and banners to make them more festive. See also **gospel procession.**

Processional Cross: Wooden or metal cross or crucifix attached to the top of a pole so that it may be carried in processions. [Figure 1]

Profession, Religious: Taking vows of poverty, chastity, and obedience and thus embracing the life of the "religious" in a monastic community.

Propers: Variable texts of a celebration of the Eucharist or an observance of the Daily Offices, as opposed to the texts that always remain the same (allowing for choice among a small number of set versions), which are called the Ordinary. The Propers consist chiefly of the Collect, the Lessons, and the variable Proper Preface.

Protestant Episcopal Church in the United States of America: One of the official names of our church; the other is, simply, the Episcopal Church.

Province: A group of geographically adjacent dioceses which form an ecclesiastical unit. There are nine provinces in the Episcopal Church. In some member churches of the Anglican communion, each province has an archbishop, but in the Episcopal Church provinces elect the bishop of one of the member dioceses as president and administrative officer of the province for a term fixed by the province. The president presides over a provincial meeting, held annually except in the years of a General Convention, which is called a synod. Like the General Convention of the church, a provincial synod has a House of Bishops and a House of Deputies. Provinces promote cooperation among member dioceses and support conference centers, colleges, and other jointly operated institutions. Otherwise, provinces have little power to affect the behavior of member dioceses. The word *province* derives from the fact that such groups of dioceses were originally organized to coincide with the provinces of the Roman Empire. Sometimes *province* means one of the national members of the Anglican communion; so, in one sense England and the United States both have more than one province, but in another sense each nation is one province.

Psalm: One of the 150 Hebrew poems that make up the Book of Psalms and are used in almost every rite of the church, notably the Daily Offices, which provide for a regular repetition of the whole Book of Psalms.

Psalter: The Book of Psalms, translated for use as a liturgical text and a part of the Book of Common Prayer (BCP, 585-808). Since the early days of Anglicanism, the Prayer Book has contained a Psalter in a different translation from the one in the current authorized Bible. The Prayer Books before the revision of 1979 used the translation of the Book of Psalms done by Miles Coverdale for the first complete English Bible (1535), a version soon superseded by other translations. The Psalter in the Prayer Book of 1979 is a completely fresh translation of the Psalms, done with a concern for the liturgical uses of the Psalter and the need for them to work with a variety of styles in musical settings.

Pulpit: Elevated stand of wood, stone, or metal from which the sermon is preached. Found on the north side of the nave in traditionally arranged churches, the pulpit may also be the place from which the Gospel is read. Some traditional churches have a lectern on the south side from which the Old and New Testament lessons are read. More contemporary churches combine the role of lectern and pulpit and provide a single reading location. Sermons are now also sometimes preached from the celebrant's chair or while the preacher is standing before the congregation in front of or behind a freestanding altar. [Plate C]

Purificator: Small square of white linen, usually embroidered with a cross, used to wipe the rim of the chalice during the reception of the wine in the Eucharist and to clean the chalice during the ablutions.

Pyx: Small gold or silver box used to store consecrated bread that is to be carried to the sick.

Quicumque Vult: Latin for "whosoever will be," the opening words of and therefore an alternate name for the Athanasian Creed (BCP, 864-65).

Figure 29.   Rabat

R

Rabat: A shirt-front, usually in black, with a clerical collar attached, which can be worn over almost any other shirt (although usually a white one). [Figure 29]

Reaffirmation: The Prayer Book of 1979 provides the opportunity for a person to mark a significant stage in the Christian journey by making a public reaffirmation of baptismal vows in the presence of the bishop. This is done by having the person engage in a period of appropriate preparation and then take part in the Confirmation rite even though he or she is already confirmed. The bishop responds by using the sentence (BCP, 419) that the Holy Spirit, having "begun a good work," may "direct and uphold" the reaffirmer "in the service of Christ and his kingdom." It is appropriate that a person participate in this rite several times in an adult faith journey.

Real Presence: Term for the affirmation that in the Eucharist Christ is really and truly present to the community through the action its members do together with bread and wine, so that, in the words of the Catechism (BCP, 859), "the sacrifice of Christ is made present, . . . in which he unites us to his one offering of himself," the bread and wine becoming for us "the Body and Blood of your Son" (BCP, 363).

Reception: Moment in the Eucharist in which the congregation receives the consecrated bread and wine (BCP, 338, 364-65).

Reconciliation of a Penitent: Also known as Confession or Penance, the service for the Reconciliation of a Penitent (BCP, 447-52) appears in two forms. Form One is shorter and contains the essential Blessing, Confession, Absolution, and Dismissal. Form Two includes these but adds sentences of Scripture, an Examination, and a Laying on of Hands; it is perhaps more appropriate for marking a major turning point in the life of the penitent. The purpose of the rite is to provide a mechanism by which one who feels that he or she, having been separated from the community through some personal action of omission or commission, can hear God's forgiveness and feel the power of God's reconciling love.

Rector: Usually, the chief sacramental officer and professional ordained person in a parish, who is called by the vestry. Other clergy who work for a parish are on the staff of the rector.

Rectory: House in which the rector lives. The term is applied most easily when the parish owns the rectory and lends it to each rector in turn. Now that many clergy are buying or renting their own houses, it remains to be seen if the term can be transferred from the semipublic parish-owned rectory to the wholly private residence of the rector.

Regular: Adjective for clergy who are members of a religious order.

Religious: Noun meaning a member of a religious order, as opposed to a person who is not in religious orders and who is thus called "secular."

Religious House: A monastery or other building that houses a chapter of a monastic or religious community.

Religious Order: A community of men and/or women bound together by their vows of poverty, chastity, and obedience and by their adherence to the rule of the order. They may be called monks, friars, or nuns, and frequently wear a distinctive garment called a habit. They may live in a special building called a monastery, priory, friary, or convent, or they may simply live communally in a house. Some religious orders live a life cut off almost entirely from the rest of the world; others take on missions of spiritual direction, retreat work, teaching, service to the poor, and the like. In the Episcopal Church today there are over thirty religious orders.

Renewal of Baptismal Vows: Rite that forms part of the Easter Vigil (BCP, 292-94) when there are to be no Baptisms. It is also recommended by the Prayer Book (BCP, 312) for Pentecost, All Saints' Day or Sunday, and the Feast of the Baptism of our Lord when no Baptisms take place. This action on the part of the congregation is also a part of Baptisms and Confirmations.

Repose, Altar of: Altar on which bread and wine consecrated on Maundy Thursday are reserved for communion on Good Friday.

Requiem: Traditional name for a celebration of the Eucharist as part of a funeral, as provided for in the Prayer Book services of Burial of the Dead (BCP, 482, 498). Traditionally the liturgical color for a requiem has been black, but we now recognize that, in the words of the Prayer Book, "the liturgy for the dead is an Easter liturgy," and so the appropriate color is white.

Reredos: Technically, any decoration put up above and behind an altar; now usually employed to mean a carved stone or wood structure behind the high altar in a traditionally arranged church. [Plate A]

Reservation: The practice of keeping consecrated bread and sometimes wine available for communion of the sick or, in some places, for devotional purposes such as Benediction of the Blessed Sacrament.

Reserved Sacrament: The consecrated bread and wine kept in reservation, usually in an aumbry in the wall of a church, or in a tabernacle on one of the altars. A sanctuary lamp is kept lighted nearby as a sign of honor and also to alert visitors to the location of the reserved sacrament. The lamp burns white when the sacrament is present, and red when it is not.

Response: Second half of the versicle/response pattern of interaction between officiant and congregation that occurs in a number of rites. In the Eucharist, for example, the celebrant's proclamation (BCP, 337, 364) "Christ our Passover is sacrificed for us" is a versicle, and the congregational part, "Therefore let us keep the feast," is a response. Versicles and responses may also be exchanged between choir and congregation, by two halves of a choir, or by a cantor and the choir.

Retable: Shelf behind the altar on which may be placed a cross, candlesticks, or other objects; another word for the gradine.

Retreat: A period of days spent away from ordinary routine, frequently in silence, and occupied in meditation or other religious exercises. Many monastic communities invite those seeking a retreat to join in their community worship routine; others provide more structured spiritual direction. The model of the time away has also found application for members of vestries or other church groups who wish to go away together to learn how to work together better. In this case the retreat may take place in a monastic setting, but the group hires a consultant to lead them in exercises intended to further organizational development. In some dioceses, the bishop and clergy spend time together on retreat one or more times a year at a conference center or other place suitable for housing large groups.

Reverence: Verb meaning to treat with special honor the altar or the blessed sacrament (if it is kept in reservation) by means of a solemn bow or genuflection.

Reverend, The: Title of address for a deacon or priest.

Reverend, The Most: Title of address for an archbishop.

Reverend, The Right: Title of address for a bishop.

Reverend, The Very: Title of address for the dean of a seminary or cathedral; also used for a rural dean or one in charge of a diocesan subdivision.

Ring: The Prayer Book requires that at a wedding at least one of the couple give the other a ring or other suitable symbol of the vows; this may be blessed by the officiant (BCP, 427). The couple may exchange rings or other symbols, which may also be blessed, but this is at the discretion of the couple. The bishop's ring is also one of the insignia of the episcopal office; frequently it contains a concave representation of the diocesan crest and can be used to make official seals in wax on ordination certificates. On occasion, nuns also receive wedding rings when they make their life professions and thus in a sense marry Christ.

Rite One: The rites of Eucharist (BCP, 319-50), Morning and Evening Prayer (BCP, 37-60, 61-74), and Burial (BCP, 469-89) which are written in a liturgical language in imitation of Elizabethan English. A comparison of the texts of these rites with the texts of the Elizabethan Prayer Book makes clear that over time the original language of the Prayer Book has been changed in a variety of ways to make it seem more appropriate for use in formal worship. The

Rite One services combine that language with the results of liturgical scholarship to produce traditional-sounding rites with the integrity that modern knowledge can bring.

Rite Two: The rites of Eucharist (BCP, 355-99), Morning and Evening Prayer (BCP, 75-102, 115-26), and Burial (BCP, 491-505) in contemporary language. For these services BCP also has a traditional language version called Rite One. The other rites, for which the Prayer Book does not offer these alternatives, are in contemporary language, with the exception of the Great Litany, which appears only in its traditional language form.

Rite Three: Unofficial term sometimes used for the Order for Celebrating the Holy Eucharist (BCP, 400-01) and the Order for Burial (BCP, 506-07), because there are Rite One and Rite Two versions of these services, and, by analogy, for the Order for Marriage (BCP, 435-36), although there is no "Rite One" version of the marriage rite in the Book of Common Prayer.

Ritual: Originally a word referring to the text of liturgical services. It has now come to refer instead to how the rites are done and is thus similar in meaning to the term *ceremonial*.

Rochet: Among the vestments distinctive to the office of bishop, the rochet is a white, shoulder-to-shoe vestment similar to an alb, except that it has wide sleeves with fluted cuffs which are puffed at the shoulders and gathered at the wrists by red or black silk bands. The rochet is worn over the bishop's purple cassock and under his chimere. [Figure 30]

Figure 30.   Bishop
             in Rochet and Chimere
             with Pastoral Staff

Rogation Days: Days on the calendar of the liturgical year, traditionally observed on the Monday, Tuesday, and Wednesday after the Fifth Sunday after Easter, the three days before Ascension Day. These days originally were for prayer for fruitful harvest and were observed by formal processions around the geographic boundaries of the parish. The Prayer Book now includes prayer for commerce and industry and for the stewardship of creation as well as for fruitful seasons (BCP, 258-59) and provides that the rogation days be observed when and how a parish finds appropriate for its situation and environs.

Rood: An ancient English word for cross. One feature of medieval church furnishings was a screen which shut off the nave from the chancel and was called a chancel screen. Often the chancel screen was topped with a beam on which rested a large crucifix or Christus Rex. In this case, the screen was called a rood screen and the beam on which the rood sat was called a rood beam. Since we no longer build chancels for the monastic chapter and naves for the laity, we no longer separate the chancel so decisively from the nave. Thus there are few chancel screens to be seen except in old English churches where they survive or have been restored. But the rood itself is a feature of many Episcopal churches, where it sometimes retains the name rood screen.

Rosary: A devotional aid especially associated with the honoring of the Blessed Virgin Mary. It is not widely used in the Episcopal Church, although some Episcopalians find it an important part of their devotional lives. The rosary consists of a string of beads divided into units of twelve. Each unit guides the person saying the rosary to begin with recitation of the Lord's Prayer (a large bead), then say ten Hail Marys (ten small beads), and conclude with the Gloria Patri (a large bead). A complete saying of the rosary involves fifteen repetitions of this unit, five devoted to the five joys, five to the five sorrows, and five to the five glories of the Blessed Virgin Mary. The five joys are the annunciation, the visitation, the nativity, presentation of Christ in the temple, and the finding of Christ in the temple. The five sorrows are the agony of Christ in Gethsemane, the scourging, the crowning with thorns, the carrying of the cross, and the crucifixion. The five glories are the resurrection, the ascension, the descent of the Holy Spirit, the assumption of Mary, and the coronation of Mary. These are also known as the fifteen mysteries of the Blessed Virgin Mary, with each unit of five called a chaplet.

Rubrics: From a Latin word meaning "red." Rubrics are directions found in the Prayer Book about the conduct of worship. They are called rubrics because at one time they were almost universally printed in red ink to make them stand out from the black type of the rites themselves. Some are found at the beginning of the rites, others are printed in italic type at various points in the rites, and others are printed in lists of additional directions at the end of the rites.

Rule: Directions for conduct of monastic life set down by the founder of a specific monastic community. Thus the life of Benedictines is guided by the Rule of St. Benedict, and the life of the Society of St. John the Evangelist is guided by the rule of its founder, R. M. Benson, set forth at Cowley, England, in 1865.

Sabbath: The seventh day of the Jewish week. Early Christians observed the Sabbath (our Saturday) as a day of rest, but because Jesus rose from the dead and the Holy Spirit came at the first Pentecost on the first day of the week, that day (Sunday) was the day for having the Eucharist at the Christian assembly. With time the two days became confused, so that some Christians thought of Sunday as the weekly day of rest. Calendars still reflect the traditional scheme, showing Saturday as the seventh day of the week and Sunday as the first day.

Sacrament: According to the Catechism, sacraments are "outward and visible signs of inward and spiritual grace, given by Christ as sure and certain means by which we receive that grace" (BCP, 857). The Episcopal Church recognizes the two sacraments of Baptism and Eucharist as biblical and as essential to the church, according to the Lambeth Quadrilateral. It also recognizes other sacramental rites which evolved in the church under the guidance of the Holy Spirit, including Confirmation, Ordination, Holy Matrimony, Reconciliation of a Penitent, and Unction of the Sick. God's activity is not limited to these sacraments, although they do form a pattern of the way in which God uses material things to reach out to us. All of these have in common an action with an object and a set of words. For instance, in Baptism the action is the pouring of water on the head and the words are the formula "I baptise you in the name of the Father and of the Son and of the Holy Spirit."

In the case of the Eucharist, the action is the offering, giving thanks, breaking, and distributing of the bread and wine, and the words are the institution narrative of the Lord's Supper. The Episcopal Church is a thoroughly sacramental church: The action which tells us who we are as Christians every Sunday is properly the Eucharist. Sacramental Christianity is at heart an understanding of God's creation and history as the arena in which God meets us and acts for our reconciliation to God, using the simple things of our material existence as signs of God's love.

Sacrament Lamp: One name for the sanctuary lamp that hangs or stands near the location of the reserved sacrament and burns white when the blessed sacrament is present and red when it is not.

Sacring Bell: Also called sanctus bell, a bell rung during the recitation of the Eucharistic Prayer to call the congregation's attention to significant moments, such as the recitation of the words of institution. In parishes where such bells are rung, it is often part of the ceremonial tradition for the priest to elevate the bread and wine in turn during the words of institution and then again together at the end of the Prayer. The ringing of this bell usually coincides with the elevation.

Sacristan: Person responsible for the things that are done in a sacristy.

Sacristy: Room close to the eucharistic room or sanctuary in which the chalice, paten, and other equipment for celebrating the Eucharist, such as purificators and altar linen, are cleaned, stored, and made ready for use.

Saint, Saints' Days: The member churches of the Anglican communion recognize in their liturgical calendars the saints mentioned in the Bible. Each member church is free to add to that list other medieval and more recent figures; for a complete list of those recognized by the Episcopal Church, see the calendar on pages 19-33 of the Book of Common Prayer. Saints in the Episcopal Church are honored as members of the cloud of witnesses to the faith with which God has surrounded us and as examples of Christian living.

Salutation: The acclamation versicle and response at the beginning of the Eucharist (BCP, 323, 355).

Sanctuary: In a traditional church building, the name for the the area around the altar, especially the space inside the altar rail.

Sanctuary Lamp: A lamp hanging in front of the altar. There may be as many as seven, although three is a more common number.

Sanctus: Latin for "holy"; thus one name for the hymn of adoration beginning "Holy, holy, holy, Lord," said or sung in the Eucharistic Prayer at the end of the Preface (BCP, 334, 362). It derives from Isaiah 6:1-3.

Sanctus Bell: See **sacring bell.**

Scapular: A garment that forms part of the regular monastic habit, the scapular is essentially a long wide band of material with an opening for the head that is worn over the shoulders and reaches almost to the feet. Usually black, it is worn with a cassock.

Seal of Confession: The absolute prohibition, which allows no exception, against a priest's or bishop's revealing anything said by a penitent using the rite for the Reconciliation of a Penitent.

Search Committee: A group selected by the vestry of a parish (or the mission committee of a mission) in consultation with the bishop. Its job is to facilitate the search for a new rector or vicar. The search committee is to be a representative group from a congregation; its membership may also include people from outside the congregation or even outside the Episcopal Church, if the wider community would be affected by the choice. The task of the search committee is to select and recommend candidates to fill the vacancy; the parish group makes its recommendations to the vestry, while the mission group answers to the bishop.

Sedilia: Latin word for "seat"; this term is sometimes used for the seat used by the celebrant. Chairs for the deacon and subdeacon and acolytes are usually found on either side of the sedilia. May also be called the president's or presider's chair.

See: From a Latin word meaning "seat," this is another word for the bishop's chair or throne, but it is more customarily thought of as meaning the geographical area in which the bishop's throne is located and thus is another word for diocese. Occasionally the city which contains the bishop's cathedral or office is called the see city of the diocese.

Seminary: An educational institution that offers programs of instruction leading to the degree of Master of Divinity (M. Div.), which is the professional degree for those seeking ordination. Some seminaries also offer the Doctor of Ministry (D. Min.), which is a professional doctorate for clergy. Some seminaries also offer academic degrees, such as the M.T.S. (Master of Theological Studies), the M.A. (Master of Arts), or Ph.D. (Doctor of Philosophy), which prepare people for teaching positions in school or college departments of religion. The Doctor of Divinity degree (D.D.) is always an honorary degree, and not an academic doctorate. The Episcopal Church has no "official" seminaries but recognizes certain accredited seminaries governed by independent boards of trustees as having a historical relationship to the church. They include the Episcopal Divinity School (Cambridge, Mass.), the General Theological Seminary

(New York, N.Y.), Berkeley Divinity School (New Haven, Conn.), Bexley Hall (Rochester, N.Y.), Church Divinity School of the Pacific (Berkeley, Calif.), the Episcopal Theological Seminary of the Southwest (Austin, Tex.), Nashotah House (Nashotah, Wis.), the Protestant Episcopal Theological Seminary in Virginia (Alexandria, Va.), the School of Theology of the University of the South (Sewanee, Tenn.), the Seabury-Western Theological Seminary (Evanston, Ill.), and the Trinity Episcopal School for Ministry (Ambridge, Pa.). There are also several diocesan seminaries and schools of theology which specialize in classes in the evening or on weekends for those who cannot attend a seminary full-time. Although the church does not support these seminaries directly, parishes are directed to give one percent of their budgets to support theological education.

Seminarian: A student at a seminary. People in a parish see the most of seminarians when they are assigned to that parish for field work, usually twelve hours a week of involvement in the life of the parish under the supervision of the rector or a member of the clergy staff. Seminarians are usually licensed to function as lay readers and lay chalice bearers. They may on occasion get to preach a sermon.

Sequence Hymn: Hymn sung between the New Testament lesson and the Gospel, during which the Gospel procession or other special ceremonial forms and moves into place.

Server: General title for anyone who assists at the altar, interchangeable with acolyte.

Service Book: The copy of the texts and music for the eucharistic rites which is used by the celebrant; also called the altar book or altar missal.

Sexton: The parish custodian, whose job is to keep the church buildings and facilities clean and in good working order.

Shell, Baptismal: Metal or ceramic cup or dish in the shape of a large sea shell used in some places to pour water during the administration of Baptism.

Shrove Tuesday: The day immediately before Ash Wednesday, named for the "shriving," or confessions and absolutions, performed traditionally in that day. Also known as Mardi Gras, or "Fat Tuesday," for those who prepare for Lent by making sure they have sins of which to repent.

Sick, Visitation of the: Another term for the rite of Ministration to the Sick (BCP, 453-61) which involves the reading of Scripture, the Laying on of Hands and Anointing, and Holy Communion. One of the special features of this section of the Prayer Book is a selection of prayers for use for and by a sick person (BCP, 458-61).

Side Altar: An altar to the side of the high altar, or the main altar; so named because the high altar in a traditional church is on the central axis of the building and other altars or chapels are thus to the side of the high altar. [Plate C]

Figure 31.   Simple Bow   Figure 32.   Solemn Bow

Simple Bow: An act of respect performed by inclining one's head and shoulders slightly; performed by some at the mention of the name of Jesus, when the processional cross passes them, at the words "Holy, holy, holy, Lord" in the Sanctus, and on other occasions. [Figure 31]

Sister: Title of a lay member of a religious order for women.

Sign of the Cross: A manual act, customary to some degree in most places, which links the cross with our claim that we experience now "all benefits of Christ's passion." There are three forms of the sign of the cross. The first is that made on the forehead of those being baptized, confirmed, or anointed with oil in healing services, proclaiming that they are "marked as Christ's own for ever" (BCP, 308). This is done by the bishop or priest using the thumb of the right hand. The second form of the sign of the cross is made in the act of blessing or pronouncing absolution by a bishop or priest, who makes the shape of a large cross in the air, first forming the vertical axis and then the horizontal axis. This may be done toward the people being blessed, or over wine, bread, or other objects. The right hand is used to make the sign of the cross with hand extended, thumb in. The fingers may be together, or one or two of the fingers farthest from the thumb may be curved inward and the thumb brought forward to touch them. The third form of the sign of the cross is made by an individual on him or herself, again using the right hand, by touching the forehead, the diaphragm, the left shoulder, and the right shoulder with the fingertips. This personal sign of the cross is made appropriately by anyone at different times in the Eucharist or in other rites. It is done by the congregation as they are being blessed by the celebrant as an act of accepting their forgiveness and blessedness. It is also done as a kind of manual "Amen" at other times, especially at the naming of the Trinity by person, at the end of the Creeds, and, by some, at the "bless us also" phrase in the Eucharistic Prayers. Some find this sign meaningful before and/or after receiving the bread and wine. Yet another form of the sign of the cross involves making a cross on the forehead, the lips, and the heart with the thumb (nail-side) of the right hand, the fingers curled inward, at the announcement "the Holy Gospel of our Lord and Savior Jesus Christ according to. . . ." before the reading of the Gospel. If the person reading the Gospel makes this sign as he or she announces it, the action is taken one step further with a fourth cross signed on the Gospel book. This fourth form of the sign of the cross is a manual way of praying that the Gospel be in my mind, on my lips, and in my heart. As in the case of any action which is learned primarily by watching others, many local variations are possible. [Figure 15]

Solemn Bow: A bow from the waist, with inclination of the head and shoulders, performed in reverence to the altar, and also, for example, at the words "became incarnate from the Virgin Mary" in the Nicene Creed. Local custom varies. [Figure 32]

Solemn Eucharist: A celebration of the Eucharist as it is done for the main service on Sundays and on the major holy days, with celebrant, deacon, and subdeacon; full vestments; music; full ceremonial; and everything else that is appropriate for the congregation to express its full understanding of the importance of the Eucharist.

Solemn Procession: A procession of the type that begins at the altar, goes down the main aisle, around the side aisles, and back up the main aisle; used chiefly on major feast days.

Song of Praise: General name for the song, hymn, or canticle that is sung or said after the opening acclamation in the Eucharist (BCP, 324, 356). The Prayer Book suggests three texts, the Kyrie Eleison, the Gloria in Excelsis, and the Trisagion; it implies that in Rite One the customary text will be the Kyrie or the Trisagion, with the possibility that the Gloria will be sung in addition to (a very traditional arrangement), or instead of, the former. In Rite Two, the suggestion is that the Gloria will be the text, with the possibility that the Kyrie or Trisagion will take its place. In neither rite is the Gloria sung during Advent or Lent. Instead of these, some other hymn from the *Hymnal* may be sung.

Sponsors: Those who present candidates for Baptism. Each candidate must have one or more sponsors, one of whom must be baptized. Sponsors of adults and older children endorse their candidacy and promise to support them in the Christian life by prayer and example. Sponsors of infants are called godparents; they present the candidates, make the baptismal promises in their own names, and also take vows on behalf of their candidates, pledging to see that they are reared in the Christian life (BCP, 298, 301-02).

Staff, Pastoral: Another term for crosier, the bishop's staff of office, which is now usually made to resemble a shepherd's crook to remind us that the bishop is the chief pastor of the diocese.

Stalls: Fixed seats for choir and clergy found in the chancels of many traditionally arranged churches. They may be called choir stalls, and can be elaborately carved and surmounted by canopies.

Stand: The object which supports the altar or service book on the altar. Also called a missal stand, it may be simply a pillow, or may be a shelf on a base made of wood or metal.

Standing Committee: Group of lay and ordained people elected by diocesan convention to serve primarily as a committee of advice and consent to the bishop. For instance, part of the job of the Standing Committee is to meet with those recommended for ordination to the bishop by the diocesan Commission on Ministry. The bishop cannot ordain

156

these people without the consent of the Standing Committee. Another part of the Standing Committee's responsibility is to consent to the consecration of a bishop in another diocese; before someone elected bishop in a diocese can be consecrated, the permission of a majority of diocesan Standing Committees must be secured. The special responsibility of the Standing Committee, however, is to stand in readiness in case the diocese is for some reason without a bishop. In that case, the Standing Committee becomes the ecclesiastical authority and takes over the bishop's diocesan administrative responsibility until a new bishop is consecrated. The Standing Committee must also approve of all sales of church property.

Station: Place in church where, during a solemn procession, there is a pause for a versicle, response, and a collect. These include the creche at Christmas, the entrance to the church on Palm Sunday, and the baptismal font on the day of Pentecost. The rite for the Station at the Christmas Creche is in the Book of Occasional Services, 34-5.

Figure 33.   Examples of Stations
of the Cross

Stations of the Cross: A series of fourteen pictures or carvings depicting incidents in the narrative of Christ's passion, from Pilate's house to the entombment, which are found arranged around the walls of some churches. They are used in conjunction with the devotional service The Way of the Cross (BOS, 55-71) in which the stations are visited in turn, with a pause for a reading, a versicle and response, a collect, and perhaps time for meditation. This devotion is especially appropriate for the Fridays in Lent. [Figure 33]

Stewardship: A steward is one who takes care of an owner's estate while the owner is away. Christian stewardship involves living out our claim that we are stewards of creation and not its owners. God made the world and entrusted it into our care, so we are responsible for what happens to it and what we do with it. In this context, we also think about our responsibility for the maintenance of the church as the sign in the world of God's redemptive love.

Stipend: The compensation package paid Episcopal clergy who work for congregations. It includes salary, housing or housing allowance, utilities allowance, and other components, but not the cost to the congregation of employing an ordained person, such as travel allowance, insurance premiums, and pension payments. Clergy who earn their wages in nonparochial employment are referred to as "nonstipendiary."

Stole: A long, narrow strip of material, often with religious symbols, which is the distinctive vestment of the deacon and

Figure 34.   Deacon in Alb
with Stole Crosswise

priest. Deacons wear the stole over the left shoulder so that it crosses the chest and back and is tied under the right arm. Priests wear the stole around the neck with the ends hanging down the front, as do bishops. When the Ordination rites refer to priests and deacons being "vested according to the order," the essential part of complying with that rubric is putting on the stole. Stoles are made in the colors of the church year and clergy wear ones appropriate for the season. Traditionally, parishes owned sets of eucharistic vestments with matching stoles. These are, of course, still worn, but the increase in the practice of concelebration and of using several clergy to help administer the bread and wine at communion has led to clergy owning their own sets of stoles, some of which are extremely fine examples of liturgical handicraft. [Figure 34]

Stoup: Basin near the entrance of a church building in which holy water is kept so that parishioners may sprinkle themselves with it, usually by making the sign of the cross with moistened fingers. This is part of the entrance ceremonial customary in some parishes. [Figure 5]

Stripping of the Altar: In some places, part of the Maundy Thursday liturgy is to remove everything from the altar or altars of the church building, including the candlesticks, crosses, "fair linen," and frontal, leaving the altars bare, except that if there is to be an altar of repose for the reserved sacrament consecrated at the Maundy Thursday Eucharist to be kept for use on Good Friday, it is not stripped. Stationary crosses or other decorations in the church are covered at the end of the Maundy Thursday ceremonies, a dramatic way of looking forward to Good Friday. It reminds us that the Eucharist is not celebrated until the Easter Vigil; in remembrance of our Lord's passion, the church's observance of the sign of his resurrection is suspended.

Subdeacon: A role in the full ceremonial for celebration of the Eucharist. The subdeacon sits and stands to the celebrant's left, while the deacon sits and stands to the celebrant's right. When full sets of eucharistic vestments are available, the subdeacon wears a tunicle. Long ago, the subdeacon was an office to which one was ordained, like the deacon, but that is no longer the case. The subdeacon is now usually a layperson, probably a licensed layreader and chalice bearer who reads the Epistle or leads the intercessory prayers. One of the most powerful actions of the church is to have a bishop or priest as celebrant, a deacon as deacon and a layperson as subdeacon, so that all the orders of ministry are represented around the altar and each order can understand its identity in terms of its functions in the Eucharist.

Suffragan Bishop: A bishop elected by a diocesan convention to assist the bishop of the diocese. A suffragan bishop differs from a bishop coadjutor in that although a coadjutor may serve as assisting bishop to the bishop of a diocese for a time, the coadjutor was elected specifically to succeed the diocesan bishop at the latter's retirement and the suffragan was not. The suffragan bishop may succeed the diocesan bishop but must be elected again by the diocesan convention specifically to do that.

Suffrages: A set of petitions stated in the form of a series of versicles and responses, especially used for the sections of such interchanges found in Morning and Evening Prayer (BCP, 55, 67-68, 97-98, 121-22) after the Lord's Prayer. The word is not limited to these occasions, however, and the form of some of these suffrages makes clear that any intercessory prayer cast in the form of versicle and response could be called suffrages.

Sunday: The day on which we remember every week Jesus' rising from the dead on the first day of the week. The Prayer Book makes clear that the Holy Eucharist is "the

160

principal act of Christian worship on the Lord's Day" (BCP, 13). Every Sunday is a little Easter, and is always a feast day. Sundays mark the passing of time in each of the six liturgical seasons, and special collects are provided for each of them (BCP, 159-85 and 211-36). On the calendar of the church year, Sundays always take precedence over the observation of any day except a few major variable holy days like Christmas Day and the Epiphany, although it is permissible for a parish to observe the Sunday after All Saints' Day as All Saints' Sunday.

Sunday of the Passion: Another name for Palm Sunday (BCP, 270), so called because on it one of the accounts of Jesus' passion is read for the first time in any Lenten season. It also begins Holy Week.

Superior: Title given to the head of some monastic communities; if male, often called father superior, and if female, mother superior. The Order of the Holy Cross and the Brotherhood of St. Gregory have superiors, and the Society of St. John the Evangelist has a father superior. The Society of St. Margaret has a mother superior, while the Order of St. Helena and the Order of St. Anne have superiors.

Figure 35.   Person in
Surplice and Tippet

Surplice: A white vestment with wide sleeves, developed from the alb, which is worn over the cassock by clergy while conducting public observance of the Daily Offices. It is worn with a tippet and occasionally an academic hood. Some clergy also wear cassock, surplice, and stole for Baptisms and for celebrating the Eucharist, although the surplice is really an Office vestment rather than a eucharistic vestment. Surplices are also worn with cassocks by lay readers taking part in the Offices and by clergy assisting at the Eucharist. [Figure 35]

Sursum Corda: Latin for "Lift up your hearts"; thus the name of the versicle and response section of the Preface in the Eucharistic Prayers which contains that line (BCP, 333, 361, and elsewhere).

Symbols: Images used as decoration on hangings, banners, vestments, stoles, altar frontals, and other places around the church or on religious jewelry. They become symbols because through association or convention we give them power to provoke profoundly rich experiences beyond what they could produce on their own. These images are usually ancient; there are many of them. Illustrated here are a few of the most common ones found on vestments. The cross with IHΣ (Figure 35a) combines the image of Christ's crucifixion with the first three letters of the word *Jesus* in Greek. The fish with the letters IXΘΥΣ (Figure 35b) derives from the fact that the first letters of the phrase "Jesus Christ, Son of God, Savior" in Greek spell the Greek word for "fish." The image in Figure 35c combines the Greek letters chi and rho, which are the first two letters in the Greek version of the word *Christ,* with the Greek letters alpha and omega, the first and last letters in the Greek alphabet ("I am Alpha and Omega, the first and the last," says the Lord). In Figure 35d, the letters INRI are the first letters of the Latin words *Iesus Nazarenus Rex Iudaeorum,* or "Jesus of Nazareth, King of the Jews." The dove descending in Figure 35e is a traditional image for the coming of the Holy Spirit. Other symbols frequently seen are different stylized versions of the cross and three inter-locking rings which represent the Trinity.

Figure 35a.   Figure 35b.   Figure 35c.

Figure 35d.   Figure 35e.

Synod: Meeting of the bishops and elected lay and clerical delegates from one of the nine provinces of the Episcopal Church. Provincial synods meet every year except the years in which the national church is having a meeting of the General Convention. They are also divided into a House of Bishops and a House of Deputies, but their role is advisory to the individual dioceses and to the General Convention, because synod resolutions do not bind their member dioceses to comply.

T

Tabernacle: A boxlike compartment for keeping the reserved sacrament on an altar. Opposed to an aumbry, which is a compartment in the wall of the sanctuary or sacristy for keeping the reserved sacrament. Parishes which keep the reserved sacrament usually have one or the other, and mark the location with a special lamp.

Table, Holy or Communion: The altar.

Te Deum: Latin for "You, God"; the familiar name for a hymn (also known as Te Deum Laudamus) which begins in translation "You are God: we praise you" and is used in the Daily Offices (BCP, 52-53, 95). Sometimes, because many splendid musical settings of the Te Deum have been written, the hymn is performed in the context of the Eucharist and is called a Solemn Te Deum.

Tenebrae: One of the special services associated with Holy Week, Tenebrae (text in BOS, 73-88) on Wednesday night involves the gradual darkening of the church by progressive extinguishing of candles while Psalms and biblical texts are being read. The building is finally in total darkness when a loud noise (recalling the earthquake during Christ's passion) is made and the last candle is brought back, lighted. The congregation leaves by its light.

Thanksgiving, General: Prayer at the close of the Daily Offices (BCP, 58-59, 71-72, 101, 125) in which God is thanked for "all your goodness and loving-kindness."

Thanksgiving, Great: Term used in the Prayer Book for the Eucharistic Prayer or Canon of the Eucharist (BCP, 333, 361, and elsewhere). The word *eucharist* really means "thanksgiving," and this prayer is at the heart of the eucharistic action, summing up what God has done and is doing for us.

Thanksgiving for the Birth or Adoption of a Child: Prayer Book rite (BCP, 439-45) which helps parents and congregation to express their thanks for the child prior to Baptism. This rite enables an emphasis on the birth itself and on the parents' joy in it, so it frees Baptism to carry the emphases appropriate to it.

Thanksgivings: A set of texts (BCP, 836-41) providing appropriate ways of giving thanks for a wide variety of gifts in a wide variety of personal and liturgical situations. Along with the prayers that precede this section of the Prayer Book (BCP, 814-35), this section is a resource for prayer and worship that is probably underused and repays richly time spent browsing around in it.

Thirty-nine Articles: See **Articles of Religion, Thirty-nine.**

Three Hours' Service: A service on Good Friday. Sometimes it incorporates the Good Friday liturgy, with meditations at appropriate points. Sometimes it consists of a series of meditations or sermons on Christ's seven last words from the cross, interspersed with hymns and prayers, timed to last for the three hours of the Lord's passion, from noon until three o'clock.

Throne, Episcopal: Another name for the bishop's chair, or cathedra, found in the cathedral. Some parishes reserve one chair, usually distinguished by its size or ornamentation, which is used only by the bishop coming to make a visitation and may also be referred to as the bishop's throne.

Figure 36.

Thurible and Boat

Thurible: The metal pot on a chain, with a movable lid and air holes, in which incense is burned. The chain allows the pot to be swung gently, releasing smoke through the holes. It is carried in processions and used to cense the Gospel book before the reading of the Gospel and the altar at the Offertory as part of the preparation for celebrating the Eucharist. It may also be swung gently during the recitation of the Eucharistic Prayer. Also called a censer or incense pot. [Figure 36]

Thurifer: One who carries a thurible; also called a censer.

Tippet: Black scarf worn around the neck so that the ends hang down the front; wider than a stole which it resembles; the tippet is, along with a cassock and surplice, part of a priest's vestments for reciting the Daily Offices. It often bears on the ends a seal of the Episcopal Church and the wearer's seminary crest. It is never worn when the priest is celebrating the Eucharist.

Tithe: Ten percent of income, the standard for giving in the Episcopal Church.

Torches: Candles in holders on poles so that they can be carried in procession by acolytes. Often used in processions into church and as part of a Gospel procession.

Tract: Sentence of Scripture said or sung in Lent in place of the Alleluia verse between the Epistle and Gospel. Also a small, brief religious publication usually found in a rack, called the tract rack, at the entrance to the church building.

Transept: In a church building which is cruciform, or shaped roughly like a cross, the transepts are the parts of the building that make up the arms or the horizontal crossbar of the cross. Since the nave and chancel run, at least theoretically, east and west, the transepts are the north and south transepts. [Plate C]

Transfiguration, Feast of the: One of the holy days defined by the Prayer Book as a feast of our Lord; celebrated annually on August 6. This feast recalls the account in Luke 9:28-36 of the disciples' seeing the glory of God shining forth in the face of Jesus.

Trinity Sunday: The first Sunday after Pentecost, and the only day in the church year to commemorate a doctrine and not a person or an event. This day remembers God's gift to us of knowledge of the divine nature.

Tunicle: The vestment worn with an alb by subdeacons; also sometimes called a tunic. It closely resembles the deacon's dalmatic; in fact, when the chasuble, dalmatic, and tunicle are all part of a coordinated set of eucharistic vestments, the only difference is that the dalmatic has one more horizontal stripe. [Figure 37]

Figure 37.   Person in
Tunicle

U

Unction of the Sick: The part of the service of Ministration to the Sick (BCP, 455-57) which involves anointing the sick with oil and the laying on of hands "by which God's grace is given for the healing of spirit, mind, and body" (BCP, 861).

United Thank Offering: Special offering collected by the Episcopal Church Women (ECW) which is given to people and agencies engaged in work important to that group.

Urn: Container for ashes used in the Burial of the Dead when the dead person has been cremated.

V

Vacancy: What a parish has when it is without a rector and is searching for one.

Veil: Square of material in liturgical colors matching the altar cloths and vestments; used to cover the chalice and paten in the "stack" before and after their use in the Eucharist. See illustration at paten. [Figure 26] The term is also used for the material used to cover crosses and other immovable church furnishings after the stripping of the altars on Maundy Thursday. Sometimes these veils are black.

Venerable, The: Title of address for archdeacons.

Veneration of the Cross: The devotional practice of paying reverence to a cross or crucifix as part of the service for Good Friday (BCP, 281-82).

Veni Creator Spiritus: Latin for "Come, Creator Spirit"; one of the hymns which may be sung just before the bishop performs the Laying on of Hands at an Ordination (BCP, 520, 533, 544).

Veni Sancte Spiritus: Latin for "Come, Holy Spirit"; the other hymn which may be sung just before the bishop performs the Laying on of Hands at an Ordination (BCP, 520, 533, 544).

Venite: Latin for "O come" and thus the familiar name for one of the canticles said or sung at Morning Prayer as part of the Invitatory before the selection from the Psalter (BCP, 44-45, 82). The Venite is based on Psalm 95.

Verger: In some places, the sexton, a parish employee who is the custodian of church buildings. In other places, parishes follow the English custom of designating a volunteer concerned with the care of the church building as the verger. This kind of verger carries a wand, or staff of office, called the "verge" and may have a ceremonial part in the conduct of worship such as to point out to lay readers where in the Bible the lessons are located.

Versicle: First half of the versicle/response pattern of interaction between officiant and congregation that occurs in a number of rites. In the Eucharist, for example, the celebrant's proclamation "Christ our Passover is sacrificed for us" is a versicle, and the congregational part "Therefore let us keep the feast" is a response. Versicles and responses may also be exchanged between choir and congregation, two halves of the choir, or cantor and choir.

Vespers: Traditionally one of the eight monastic hours, vespers was combined with other afternoon and evening Offices into Evening Prayer by Archbishop Cranmer. The Prayer Book's service An Order of Worship for Evening now makes it possible for a person or community to observe a vespers service either separate from or in conjunction with Evening Prayer (BCP, 109-14). The Noonday, Vespers, and Compline rites differ from the Prayer Book's Morning and Evening Prayer in that they are much shorter and simpler rites, with brief excerpts from the Bible and the Psalter. There is no effort to provide an extensive course reading of the Bible in these rites as there is in the two Daily Offices.

Vessels, Sacred: General term for the containers used in the Eucharist, that is, the chalice and paten or bread tray and the ciborium.

Vestments: Special items of clothing worn by clergy and layfolk in the conduct of public worship. For the Daily Offices these are the cassock, surplice, and tippet. For the Eucharist, they include the alb, amice, cassock-alb, girdle, stole, chasuble, dalmatic, tunicle, and cope. The bishop also has special vestments, including the rochet, the chimere, and the mitre. Each of these is discussed and illustrated in more detail in its own entry. Here, however, it might be worth noting that each of these vestments has its own special history. Many are stylized adaptations of ancient Roman street clothing which have been preserved in the usage of the church because they became identified with worship. Some people through the years have objected to vestments; others have invested them with all sorts of imposed and contrived symbolism. Now perhaps we can simply enjoy the use of vestments as a use of art and craft to enrich our worship.

Vesting Room: Room where vestments are stored and put on by those who will participate in leading worship. "To be getting vested" means to be in the vesting room putting on one's vestments. Sometimes the vesting room is also the sacristy; sometimes it is called the vestry.

Vestry: Group consisting of the rector of a parish and layfolk elected by the congregation at the annual parish meeting to be the legal governing and decision-making group in the parish. This group is called the vestry because at one time it customarily met in the vestry of the church (see **vesting room**). It is the vestry's responsibility to be the final decision-making body which hires the rector, approves the parish budget, makes parish policy decisions, and spends the parish's money. Vestry membership usually rotates among members of the congregation. Each vestry has a senior warden, often nominated by the rector, and a junior warden, both elected from among members of the vestry either by the congregation or by the vestry itself. The senior warden is to be the spokesperson of the vestry, while the junior warden is to be responsible for buildings and grounds. Vestries are usually organized into commissions or committees. In the case of a committee system, each vestry member is the chair of a committee of nonvestry members. With a commission system, two or three members of the vestry are members of each commission, along with interested nonvestry members. The difference is that with the commission system the vestry members share in running a small number of groups providing recommendations to the vestry, while with the committee system the vestry members each have a central area of responsibility. Each parish chooses its own way of structuring its vestry.

Via Media: Latin for "middle way"; a claim sometimes made for the Episcopal Church and Anglicanism in general. Since the Episcopal Church has bishops, priests, and deacons and is a sacramental church, it is something like the Roman Catholic Church. On the other hand, it stresses the importance of the Bible as a test for doctrine and encourages individual responsibility in ethical desision-making, so it is somewhat like Protestant churches. It therefore may be said to follow a middle way between the Catholic and Protestant traditions and perhaps form a bridge between them. Some people find this a helpful approach, but it causes us to think of the Episcopal Church in terms of Roman *or* Protestant categories, not in terms of the understandings of the Christian faith particular to Episcopalians or of our unique experience with and reflection on the faith. While other traditions stress the importance of authority in matters of belief or of special experiences of God's favor, we understand that grace comes in our common life together enabled by the Prayer Book. Thus our uniqueness makes us the kind of church we are, not just what we have in common with other traditions.

Vicar: The priest-in-charge at a mission, a congregation dependent financially on the diocese. The bishop of the diocese is technically rector of all missions, and the one who is resident at a mission as a substitute for the bishop is the bishop's vicar. The words *vicar* and *vicarious* both derive from the Latin word *vicarius*.

Vicarage: Place where the vicar lives.

Vigil: A nighttime service of prayer and the reading of Scripture in anticipation of a major feast day, often ending with the Eucharist. The chief one is the Great Vigil of Easter (BCP, 285-95), but the Prayer Book also provides for a vigil for Pentecost (BCP, 227) and one prior to a funeral (BCP, 465-66). The Book of Occasional Services provides rites for vigils for Christmas (BOS, 33), for the Baptism of Our Lord (BOS, 49-50), for All Saints' Day (BOS, 104-05), and for Baptism (BOS, 126).

Visitation, Episcopal: The regular visit by a bishop to a parish or mission, frequently the occasion for Baptisms and Confirmations. It is technically an opportunity for the bishops to inspect the conduct of temporal and spiritual affairs in the congregations under their care. Diocesan bishops are required by canon law to visit every congregation in their care at least once every three years.

Visitation, Feast of the: Feast celebrated May 31 which commemorates the visit paid by Mary to Elizabeth recorded in Luke 1: 39-56.

Visitation of the Sick: Traditional name for the service of Ministration to the Sick (BCP, 453-61), which includes prayer and the reading of Scripture, Laying on of Hands and Anointing, and the Eucharist.

Votive Lights: Candles lighted before a statue of our Lord or a saint in conjunction with prayer for a special need or purpose.

Vows: Solemn, voluntary promises to behave in the future in certain ways. In the church the most important are the vows taken at Baptism and affirmed at Confirmation, the vows of Marriage, and the vows of poverty, chastity, and obedience taken by those entering the monastic orders.

Wafer: Name for the thin, disklike form in which unleavened bread for communion is produced. Wafers usually come wrapped in packages of fifty. They are frequently imprinted with a crucifix or other symbol.

Wardens, Senior and Junior: Members of the vestry elected by the vestry or congregation to fulfill special duties. The junior warden is responsible for the maintenance of buildings and grounds, while the senior warden is the senior layperson in the parish, who speaks for it when that is necessary. The senior warden is often nominated by the rector.

Washing of the Altars: The washing of altars by the clergy and servers in preparation for their use at the Easter Vigil, after the altars are stripped on Maundy Thursday; part of the ceremonial in some places.

Washing of Feet: Rite performed in some places on Maundy Thursday in commemoration of Jesus' washing the feet of his disciples at the Last Supper; see BCP, 274; BOS, 91.

Watch: Another name for a vigil.

Water: One of the two parts by which Baptism is administered ("by water and the Holy Spirit"). The Thanksgiving over the Water (BCP, 306-07) summarizes the importance of water for Christians, especially the water of Baptism. Thus some parishes always have blessed water available to be used as part of the entrance into the church.

Way of the Cross: The devotion (BOS, 55-71) associated with the stations of the cross. An individual or a group pauses for prayer, versicle, and response, and the reading of Scripture at a series of up to fourteen depictions of events in the narrative of Christ's passion, placed along the walls of the church. This devotion is especially appropriate for the Fridays in Lent.

Wedding Ring: The Prayer Book requires that one member of the couple give the other a ring or other symbol "as a sign of the vows by which this man and this woman have bound themselves to each other" (BCP, 427).

Whitsunday: Traditional name for the Feast of Pentecost, so called because white used to be the color of garment in which people were baptized and Pentecost was a day in which many were baptized, making the day white with baptismal garments.

Wine: The fermented juice of grapes, essential to the celebration of the Eucharist in the Episcopal Church. Traditionally a small amount of water is mixed with the wine in the chalice at the preparation to dilute the wine (BCP, 407).

Word of God: The first part of the rite of Holy Eucharist, consisting of the preparatory acclamation, collect for purity, song of praise, Collect for the Day, the Lessons, Sermon, Creed, Prayers of the People, Confession, and Peace (BCP, 323-32, 355-60). It is followed by the Holy Communion.

Words of Institution: The repetition of the narrative of Jesus' institution of the Eucharist, which is at the heart of every eucharistic prayer.

Worship: As we experience it in the Episcopal Church, not simply adoration or praise of God, but taking part in the redemptive actions of God in Christ in human history. The "regular services appointed for public worship in this

Church" according to the Prayer Book (BCP, 13) are the "Holy Eucharist, the principal act of Christian worship on the Lord's Day and other major Feasts, and Daily Morning and Evening Prayer." The Eucharist is an action which is done together by a community to proclaim the Lord's death until he come, in which the entire Christian community "participates in such a way that the members of each order within the Church, lay persons, Bishops, Priests, and Deacons, fulfill the functions proper to their respective orders." The Offices provide for the regular reading of the Scriptures. In both kinds of worship, God speaks to us through the Bible, through prayer, and through our actions together, reminding us of God's love for us and call to us to join in the redemptive work of reconciling the world to God.

Y

YAHWEH: The personal name of God, which appears two times in the Psalter in the Prayer Book (Psalm 68:4 and Psalm 83:18) and once in the canticle "The Song of Moses" (BCP, 85). In the Old Testament, it is represented by Hebrew letters usually transliterated as YHWH, with no indication of how to pronounce them. This is called the tetragrammaton. The Old Testament often uses two other words, *Elohim* ("God") and *Adonai* ("Lord"), in conjunction with or instead of YHWH, to get around the need to pronounce the personal name of God. One attempt to pronounce and to spell YHWH produced the form *Jehovah* by combining an older transliteration of the tetragrammaton as JHVH and the vowels from the Hebrew word *Adonai*. The spelling *Yahweh* is the result of recent scholarship. The Prayer Book honors the Hebrew reticence and reverence for the name of God by using *Lord* or *Lord God* except in these three cases where the the context requires the use of *Yahweh*.

Year, Church: The church year (BCP, 15-18) has six seasons: Advent, Christmas, Epiphany, Lent, Easter, and Pentecost. It is structured in relationship to the two major feasts—Christmas, with its fixed date, and Easter, with its movable date. The Advent season begins with the First Sunday of Advent, which is always four Sundays before Christmas. The Christmas season runs for twelve days from December 25 until January 6, which is the Feast of the Epiphany. The Epiphany season follows, lasting until Ash

Wednesday, forty weekdays and six Sundays before Easter. The date of Easter, which is the first Sunday on or after the first full moon after the vernal equinox (March 21), can move between March 23 and April 25. It thus determines the length of the Epiphany season as well as the Pentecost season, which begins with the Feast of Pentecost, fifty days after Easter. The Pentecost season then extends for a variable number of Sundays until the year begins again with the First Sunday of Advent.